I heard the sound of silence

For Rabbi Mark Schiftan,
who, as a wonderful teacher
doesn't know all the answers—
either, just the ones that
matter!
    with love and gratitude,
        Olivia Schneider Newman

I heard the sound of silence

✦

Are we related?

A Memoir

By Livia Schneider
Written in memory of my brave mother

Writer's Showcase
New York Lincoln Shanghai

I heard the sound of silence

Are we related?

Writer's Showcase
an imprint of iUniverse, Inc.

For information address:
iUniverse, Inc.
2021 Pine Lake Road, Suite 100
Lincoln, NE 68512
www.iuniverse.com

ISBN: 0-595-25937-5 (pbk)
ISBN: 0-595-65449-5 (cloth)

Printed in the United States of America

FOR

BOTICOMONIRAVI

Contents

Part I

Striving for Equanimity
Through the Colors of Life,
Finding Light in Darkness,
Searching for the Real Meaning,
Looking for Solace beyond the Pain,
Touching your Unknown Self,
Wishing for Wholeness,
Praying for Relief,
Receiving tikvah, Hope…

Hearts that have known pain meet in mutual recognition and trust. Such a meeting helps immeasurably. Ram Dass

◆   ◆   ◆

There is a saying that everything happens for a reason; and I am a perfect example for this saying...I found the reason...

At first I was very angry when this freak accident occurred.

I was angry at those people who had let it happen, angry, that they had not covered this I-beam I was bumping into while stepping back from the check out-counter of a local office supply store.

I was angry for a long time after being in so much pain caused by this injury that I became a hermit.

I was angry that I was left unable to work, to do the work I loved most: to paint, sew and knit, those were the skills needed to pursue my business. It was my hands that were primarily affected by this intractable pain!

I was angry to not be able to be with my family, unable to hold my grandkids, unable to be with my friends, go to meetings or art openings.

Actually, I guess, I was angry that fate had struck me with a chronic pain condition for that nobody had yet found a cure!

But then, after several years, I realized that anger, frustration and self pity did not get me anywhere, neither would it ease my pain...

I started to scold myself for having lost so much time by giving in to anger, frustration and self-destructive thoughts.

There must be an other way to get my life back!

I started to meditate, think positively and turn my pity toward those who are much worse off than I; and I succeeded to a certain degree. Given a new medication I got my pain under some control and want to keep it there, until there will be a cure. And I have high hopes for that to happen!

I definitely do not want to waste more time on dwelling what I have lost for now, but want to create my future by finding all the hidden secrets of my past…

That's what made me start to research my heritage…and, by looking through my late mother's journals, I found the PURPOSE…

Explore daily the will of GOD
Carl Jung

◆   ◆   ◆

I was supposed to be born in Haifa. That's all I knew growing up, and never asked my mother, why.

I only knew the reason why I was not born in Haifa: because the doctor did not allow my mama to travel that far while she was pregnant with me. I just took it as a fact, like I took it as a fact that I was born in Vienna, Austria, instead. And as I took it as a fact that my father had died when I was still too young, to remember.

But I always felt that there was something missing…!

Though I was born in Vienna 1938, I grew up in war-torn Hamburg, Germany, where my mama took me in a hurry after she told me that my Tate had passed away. Where did he go to? Why could he leave me?

He was there in the morning, wasn't he? When we left to go to Tante Feldscharek, he did kiss me good-bye…

I do not remember that he had been sick, and if there was anything else my mama told me…I just missed him; and I was confused and sad.

There was only the long train ride and many loud soldiers on the train and we did not have any luggage, and I was holding on to my doll that I had received at my last birthday from Tate…

The year was 1941.

I had never heard anyone else call their father Tate, but Mama told me that was just a pet name for him and I should keep it a secret, one, that only we shared. So, I did…

Yet, I still had the feeling that there was something else I was not supposed to know about him, something that happened to my father. I remembered him, remembered and missed him. I missed him tucking me in at night, and talking to me in a very soft voice…telling me stories about God and singing wonderful melodies—he was laughing and teasing me, and his beard was wiggling, and then Mama started laughing too…

I also missed Bobetchi and Opapa. They were my grandparents who were with us quite often. They might even have lived with us in our house sometimes, or we in theirs; and all my aunts, uncles and cousins; I missed them too. And then there was Uncle Jacob the shoemaker. I remember that he was a shoemaker because when we were singing this children's song: *Im Keller ist es duster, da wohnt ein armer Schuster*…meaning: in the dark basement there lives a poor shoemaker…when one cousin of mine used to say: like Uncle Jacob.

I was especially close to Aunt Leah and Aunt Lotti. Aunt Lotti used to give me dried orange rind, which I did not like at first but later always asked for when I was with her. There was this special taste, this sweet and bitter taste I did not have later for a very long time.

Why did they not come with us?

…sometimes I thought that all those people lived only in my imagination, that it was wishful thinking of a small child whose life had changed so drastically from one moment to the other, from being in a warm caring family to running away, running away from what, from whom? And not knowing what was real and what was maybe just imagination, fed by those pictures I used to see of us as a family, of Mama, Tate and me, taken on various locations, and some inside or outside our house in Vienna…those pictures were so much alive in my mind, it always felt like they were about to jump out of their frames, and we all would be together again…and I were still a three year old child!

Where had all those pictures gone? I know some of them were sad pictures. Pictures of a family that looked as if something very tragic had happened; only I seemed to have a faint smile on my face…was it because of me, that they were sad? What was going on then?

But then it never occurred to me that my parents looked old; they could have been my grandparents. That's something, I only remembered as I grew older and found photographs of my parents before I was born. Even then they were not a young couple, but they smiled and looked happy! They were about the same height when standing together, only about five feet, not more…

And later, in Hamburg, people were asking if I had fun being with my grandma, and I remember to have always vigorously set matters straight, telling those people that this was my mama!

However, then I can remember something else vividly: that terrible noise that woke us up at night, every night, that made us run to the nearest bunker, where so many other people were running to also, and where we had to wait for hours and hours, hearing bombs falling all around us.

Sometimes the whole bunker, several stories high, was shaking, and all the people started screaming, some even prayed, they had their hands folded and looked up to the ceiling of the bunker, whispering, mumbling or crying out loud. Already then I had recognized that you can also scream without anyone hearing you making your scream only sound in your mind and for God to hear.

I knew that God was everywhere, and my mama prayed with me sometimes at night. Later I prayed alone; I even told God all my problems when Mama did not have time for me. I felt far more at ease to speak to God than to my mama. She was always so serious and sad, and never had an answer when I asked her why. From God did I not get an answer either, but that was all right; I knew, He had heard me.

One night the warning for an air raid to come was very close to the time when those so called *Christmas trees* started falling, and most people panicked on their way to the bunker. There was such a big crowd in front of the big bunker—so many people who did not want to wait!

They stumbled over a child and stomped him to death.

Mama and I just barely made it inside…all the other people behind us were turned away, had to go into the cellars of the surrounding houses.

Inside the bunker, Mama realized that she had lost our precious heavy blanket in the crowd.

Hours later when the raid was over after an other terrible ordeal, Mama dared to ask if our blanket had been found, and, sure enough, some one had turned it in!

When we left the bunker that night, none of the surrounding houses was still standing—all we could see, was rubble, dust and smoke…I still can recall the smell, that terrible stench…

How I wish that this had only happened in my imagination! But it was reality, bitter reality.

◆   ◆   ◆

Then came the time, when we had to stay in the bunker days and nights in a row, but Mama told me in a hushed voice, when I would be so frightened that my whole body trembled, that she knew the war would be over soon, just a few more days, she whispered, just a few more days…

I know she was listening every day to the radio, held her ear close to it, so nobody would hear it from outside the apartment…there were always people in our neighborhood who were supposed to keep an eye on all the tenants in our house, and who made sure that everybody had followed the rules to darken the windows and to go to the bunkers or at least into the cellars, leaving their doors open. Those people were called *Blockwarts.*

For this time we had to stay in the bunker, we received extra rations of butter, milk and bread, and the grown-ups even got extra cigarettes.

And Mama was right: the war ended only a few days later. And everybody in our house was celebrating; even Mama laughed and seemed to be happy…the first time I had seen her laugh since we had come to Hamburg.—

◆   ◆   ◆

I remember all those soldiers. Mama told me that they were British soldiers, and they had saved us, and had ended the war together with soldiers from other countries, like America, France and Russia.

I was now seven years old, had not yet gone to school, for they were all closed during the war. My mama had taught me how to read, write and work with numbers, and some other things too, besides not to get too close to strangers, not even the neighbors in our house.

I never questioned her about those things, because she was always right, she knew that the war would be over in a few days, when she told me so, and it was true.

When we first arrived in Hamburg, we had to stay with a friend of my mother's for a short while until we moved into a very small apartment right under the roof.

Mama's friend, Frau Kleiner—what a funny name, I thought Mrs. Smaller!—had a big black cat, Moritz, a very special cat who really would use the bathroom as people do sitting on the commode. Moritz did not like the pompons on my knee heights and always tried to chew them up.

When we moved into our apartment my mama had to start working during daytime and I was to stay in a preschool where I had to sleep on two chairs moved together which was very uncomfortable. I do not remember other kids sleeping that way.

One day I had to be taken to the children's hospital. I had rheumatic fever. I was to stay there for a long time. I remember to have looked through a window on one side of my room close to my bed.

Through this window I saw many little children, even babies who were infected with polio.

After the air raids increased all children were supposed to be evacuated to a safer place, called the Silent Valley.

My mama did not want me to be moved; then she would not be able to visit me every day. So she took me home out of the hospital's care at her own risk.

One day later the whole hospital was destroyed in an air raid and all the children and nurses were dead! Was it only Mama's premonition?

Then Mama's Cousin Hanna would come to stay with us and watch me while Mama was working in a public library. Mama always brought me new books to read. I did not miss playing with other kids in our house. They had made fun of me when we first met them. They made fun of how I would speak in my Austrian dialect. Therefore I rather played alone or with Lora, my parrot, or I did some drawings and reading.

I have to talk about Lora: Frau Simons, a sixty-eight year old neighbor in our apartment building was the only one Mama let me visit. She had a parrot. I right away fell in love with this feathered wonder that could talk and laugh and do a lot of funny things. Frau Simons had received Lora from her fiancé when she was eighteen; that made Lora already 60!

One day, not very long after we moved to our apartment, Frau Simons asked Mama and me if I could take care of Lora; she had to go and look after her old mother. Mama let me take Lora in and she became my best friend. Frau Simons never came back, and we never heard from her again.

Lora was always with me; I had to stay in bed most of the time unless we had to go to the cellar. The other people did not want Lora to be down there, although she was in her cage. She did not appreciate to be in her cage anyway. When no one was visiting, it rarely happened that we had visitors, I let her sit on my pillow and taught her new words and new acrobatics. She did her acrobatics on a wooden cooking spoon, twirling around it, letting her body fall back, holding on to the spoon with either her feet or her beak, and enjoying the upside down panorama; then grapping the spoon with her beak and sitting upright again, hurrahing. Lora was really a very smart parrot. She had a beautiful plumage; her front head was yellow slowly blending with turquoise and blue into a green body of different shades finishing up with lots of rainbow colored tail feathers. She had quite a large vocabulary; and she was learning very fast. Very soon she would say my name.

After I was feeling a little better Mama sometimes let me go with her to the library and I was allowed to use an old typewriter in a small storage room, where I would sit and write silly little poems. I enjoyed writing poetry, because I loved reading it too. After reading my literary expressions, Mama told me that Tate had been a poet, a real philosopher and poet. That was one of the few times she talked about Tate.

And I had one special human friend besides Cousin Hanna. This friend was invisible to others, but to me he was real. I would read to him and draw pictures for him, would even make paper dolls, boy and girl and dressed them, and we would play house.

During those air raids when Mama was at work and I could not join her, cousin Hanna would take me to the bunker, but at night after Mama had come home safely, she would sit down at my bed, and I knew that she was scared, but happy that we were together again, and so was I.

I do not remember though, Hanna being with us at night during those air raids.

After the war was over, Cousin Hanna had to leave us to care for her sick sister, and I was left home alone during Mama's working hours. I had my own key hanging on a cord around my neck, and Mama wrote daily notes, listing all the chores I had to do.

Now we did not have to fear those constant alarms anymore, but we had to struggle to find enough to eat. Everything was rationed, we were used to that during wartime, but now the rationing was even stricter, we only received stamps for very little food every month, and being only the two of us, it was very hard to survive on that.

And Lora had to stay on a very strict diet too, because her favorite food, sunflower seeds, was very hard to come by. Only if some nice colleagues of Mama's have had sunflowers growing in their yards we would indulge her. Otherwise she had to eat what we could spare which was not much; she always first looked what we had on our plates. When there was anything different from what she got, she threw her dry bread down and asked if she could get something else. It really was funny! She asked:" And what does Lora get?" Only when she received whatever we had she was satisfied.

For a short time my mama went back to her former job, working as nurse during night time, but she also kept her day job. She was working on the floor were all those people, mostly very young ones, with tuberculosis had their rooms. They got a very good diet. Most of them were too sick to even touch their food. Then Mama would bring those returns home, scratching the butter from the bread and heating it, always praying that I might not get infected.

In the long run it was just too much for Mama to work two jobs and at the same time risk my health.

After a few months she quit that position, and we had to do without butter schmalz.

I missed cousin Hanna, who was a daughter of Mama's oldest sister, but since she was over thirty years older than I, I never thought of her as my first cousin.

I did not only miss her being around, what I missed the most was the way Mama and she have been talking when we were alone. I could not understand everything, and pretended to not understand anything at all, because Mama told me that this was an East Prussian dialect, and if I ever should be able to understand it, I would not be allowed to stay and listen while they were talking, for it was some low dialect and no educated children should speak that way. She did not tell Lora though, since she repeated words to me Mama and Cousin Hannah had spoken before.

And this dialect sounded so beautiful and warm, nothing like that harsh North-German people were speaking in Hamburg!

I especially loved it when Mama and Hanna would sing in that dialect, I could have listened all night long to the wonderful soprano of Hanna's and Mama's alto voice in harmony…

Those few years with Cousin Hanna made me feel safer, even during war time than the unfriendly and hostile environment after the war.

When I was haunted by nightmares, hearing those war sirens, I just had to think of Hanna and Mama singing, and mostly I could go back to sleep and dream of Tate playing with me.

◆   ◆   ◆

Everything was destroyed; women were trying to salvage from the rubble what could be saved. Stone by stone would be turned over, the dirt removed and the cleaned ones would be piled up.

Sometimes on my way to the grocery store or the farmer's market I dared to stop and watch them do this awful cleaning up job, but it never took long until some one would yell at me and ask me what I was staring at, calling me names, like carrot head or red witch…So, I knew they did not like being observed by anyone, not even a small girl who was just curious…

I always had to wait in a long line wherever I was to buy anything with my stamps. Bread in a bakery, but only heavy yellow corn bread, nothing else there. At the butcher's most of the time you could not get anything, not even with those few stamps, and the grown-ups were always trying to cut in line, asking for some extra fat. Nobody cared that I stood there and waited all along; it was a terrible feeling being on my own all alone in a cruel grown-up world! I thought it unjust that all the women were served first.

At the milk shop I would be given a quarter of a liter whole milk a day, and sometimes the shop owner would fill my little extra can with some blue milk, or butter milk. She liked me.

At the farmer's market it was a different story; we did not have stamps for produce, but some days I was lucky to be the first arriving at dawn and bringing home some cabbage or yellow turnip.

While standing in line was very boring, I overheard several conversations that did not make any sense to me. But when I later asked Mama about the meaning of some she always had this sad look on her face.

One phrase stuck to me forever, and I only learned later, much later, what it meant: *If it had not been for all those money seeking, dirty, greedy Jews, this terrible war would have never happened and my husband would be still alive.* There was some kind of understanding between those women, however, some did not agree. They meant that it was all Hitler's fault…

When I asked Mama who those Jews were, she only shook her head, turned away and did not answer me. Maybe she did not know either!…But that was not her normal behavior, she usually would answer all my questions one way or the other…but whom could I ask?

I had to get water from the wagon that came always at different times. I had to stand in line there too, but then I had trouble carrying the bucket upstairs, one step at a time; water was precious and not to be wasted…there was nothing coming out of the faucets anymore. Same was with electricity and gas. We had to use carbide lamps. Everybody owned them. They had been useful during power outages while the war was going on; but why now? Mama told me, that everything had to be rationed. Everything had to last longer until the country would be back to its former state. She got a little metal stove traded in for lots of cigarettes she had collected all those years, and now we had to find wood or anything else that would burn in this mixture between oven and stove, to cook on and to keep us warm.

◆   ◆   ◆

But there are also nice images coming up in my memory, images of a British soldier who gave me my first candy bar, Cadbury was written on it, when I was walking carrying my doll. I remember to have taken her everywhere; it would make me feel to be not so alone, standing in lines waiting to be waited on.

This tiny chocolate square would last a long time; and I had taken it in spite of Mama's warning to not get close to strangers, but I thought that this was not a common stranger, he was one of those who had saved us, and that would sooth my conscience at least a bit. And, besides, he had given me a cigarette to give to my mama. I could understand a little, when he tried to explain to me that he had a small daughter like me at home in England.

But it was very hard to really understand what he tried to tell me; that's when I decided that I had to learn English...

When Mama came home for lunch that day, I would tell her about that nice man, would show her the chocolate and give her the cigarette, and then I would explain my decision to learn his language.

Mama did not have time to teach me, so I would try it on my own. I asked her to bring me one of those books that showed the meaning of German words in English...she got one from her library, and I was eager to get started...

What I did not know, was that the pronunciation was totally different...

So, my first attempt to learn English, failed…but I was not yet giving up. I had to learn it! I wanted to talk to my new friend…I knew he was now staying in a former coffee shop not far from our house with a lot of other soldiers—

I did not even know then what a coffee shop was, but the old sign over the door read *Cafe*—I would go there once in a while, always carrying my doll, pointing at things and asking him or the other soldiers how they called those items. Then I would repeat those words until I knew them by heart. Later, at home, I would try to find the same words in my dictionary. Now I could at least say a few words in English…I was so sad that I could not carry that big book, it would have been so much easier to learn that way!

Lora would repeat a lot of those words. To her it did not make a difference what language she heard, she just copied it. She had a very strange saying though which I never understood, she must have heard it from Frau Simons; it sounded a little like Mama and Cousin Hanna used to speak. But Lora already said it before Hanna ever came." Gut schabes", she shouted every so often, but I did not know what it meant. Mama did not know either, she said.

◆　　　◆　　　◆

Mama used to prepare the food for lunch the night before, peeling potatoes, perhaps cleaning some vegetable, and it always was our main meal…I only had to remember to set the potatoes on the stove at a certain time for them to be cooked when Mama came home for her short break…and potatoes were mostly all we would have, until we would not even get those anymore.

During the war I had received some more dolls from Mama's co-workers or friends, and some very special ones from Cousin Hanna. I even had a stroller for my favorite doll; the one Tate had given me.

All those dolls and the stroller and everything else I had to play with were now considered barter objects.

Mama and I would walk miles over miles to the surrounding villages; we would knock at farmer's doors and ask them if they would be willing to part with some of their edibles in exchange for my toys, my outgrown clothes or shoes. By then the farmers were not selling their harvest at the market anymore, they had much better chances to get everything they needed in exchange for it.

Sometimes we were lucky to get some eggs or fruit, or we would be asked to pick peas for the farmer over the weekends. For one hundred pounds of fresh peas, we were to receive one pound as salary. Mama would always carefully spread out the hard earned peas on paper on the attic floor, after removing the shells.

Every tenant had access to a small stall in the common attic, only divided by light wooden slates. After there had been stolen several pounds of peas or self dug-out potatoes, Mama had to store those treasures in our living room.

But there were other times when we had walked for so long and would come home empty-handed and exhausted and hungrier than ever. I remember to have cried most nights because I could not fall asleep with my stomach protesting.

One funny thing happened though, which was not funny at all at that time. Mama rushed in one day, totally excited, that she should be able to get five pounds of sugar from one man on the street that had approached her. He was asking a lot of money for that, almost four hundred marks. Mama had only to get the money and would storm out of the door.

When she came back, red-faced and breathless, because she could have gotten caught, she was holding a big brown bag.

The top of the bag was covered with about a quarter pound of brown, wet sugar, nicely parted by a piece of paper from the rest of the bag's content, salt, salt, five pounds of salt!

First we were in shock that Mama had been taken in so easily by a stranger, but then Mama grinned and told me that we never knew when that salt would come in handy.

She had learned her lesson, and she was right. Later there was a time when you could not even buy salt anymore...

◆   ◆   ◆

All of the sudden there was white bread on the shelves of the bakery. And also white rolls! Once a month, after we received our rationing sheets that entitled us to buy some bread and butter, Mama would let me buy ten white rolls and this little bit of butter we had stamps for and we would eat up everything, a whole month worth of bread and butter stamps! That was the only time we really could eat until we were too full to get out of my bed, where we had munched for several hours, not even minding the cold temperature. Even Lora was content after she had her fill.

Money could not buy anything anyway; every one had money, because it was of no value. Cigarettes were the most sought after currency. Mama had already exchanged all her jewelry for English cigarettes.

You could get almost anything when you paid with cigarettes in addition to the regular price. If there were shoes in need of repair, Mama would put a cigarette into one shoe, and the shoemaker understood the urgency.

◆   ◆   ◆

That winter some schools opened, and Mama had to enroll me in one elementary school that was not too far away from our neighborhood.

The classes were overcrowded, almost fifty girls in one classroom. And we had to keep our coats and caps on, because there was no heat.

Mama managed somehow to get me into the third grade, nobody noticed at that time, nobody even asked our age.

By now there were so many people with children who had fled from the eastern part of the country, running away from the Russians.

There were five apartments on every floor of our four story house. All the apartments were small, no one had a bath or a shower stall; only the commode in a tiny room. To wash your hands afterward, you had to go into the kitchen. But since there was no running water, we kept a little in a wash bowl…it had to last several days though.

We were only two, plus Lora, and I tried to imagine how all our neighbors were handling this problem, some of those apartments housed five or more people.

And everyday more people were arriving. They looked even worse than we did. There was no obese person to be seen. All of them were women and children.

The only men in the neighborhood were either very old or those former *Blockwarts*, who now rather tried to be invisible; but their families always were the first to have to take in the refugees, sometimes large families…

◆   ◆   ◆

I learned from one of the older girls who now lived next door, that their apartment had originally belonged to an other family. She did not know what had happened to that family, but they still kept their furniture in the attic; maybe they would come back?

When I told my mama about that, she again shook her head and said very sadly, that those people like many others would never come back to claim their furniture.

I asked her how she knew that, but she just shrugged her shoulders as if to shrug off a load, something, she did not want to talk about because it was too awful, something only she knew and did not want to share, not even with me, her daughter. I think children have a special antenna to receive warnings about asking questions that deem detrimental.

It was not until I learned about the concentration camps and the Holocaust that I knew what had happened to those families, but that, too, was much, much later…

◆   ◆   ◆

Meanwhile I had become friends with this girl, who had fled from the East with her mother and two siblings. Her father was still a prisoner of war in a Russian camp.

Lotti and I went to school together; we were sitting together in class, where we only would receive our homework, until the heating system was restored.

But we received something else besides homework. We got food at school, hot soup, and we were told that this was from American Quakers. Nobody knew the meaning of Quakers then, but the soup was always good, and we could take it home in our cans we had to bring. We also received small bottles of cod liver oil, a terribly smelling and even worse tasting liquid we had to take a tablespoon of every day. Mama told me that children had to take it to strengthen their bones, but I sure hated it!

That winter, Mama did something very strange: she used a little of this terrible oil to cook latkes in. Those latkes were made out of raw potatoes, she would first peel and then grate them add some other ingredients and, when available one egg, and then spoon this batter into the hot oil. It smelled as terrible as or even worse than when I had to take it by spoon, ugh! How could Mama do that?

She told me that in lieu of real oil she had to use this to follow a tradition she had been following during all her life. It was then that I realized that they must have had a lot of special customs in earlier times.

I recalled that Mama and cousin Hanna were always having a peculiar way to celebrate Friday nights: cousin Hanna would set the table in a certain way, every Friday the same, she used to set those two candleholders onto the table, which she had brought with her when she came to stay with us, although we did not have any candles to put into them, it was like a ritual, everything had to be right, and I did not comprehend the purpose of this ritual. But they were pretending to light imaginary candles and sang in a language I did not understand at all.

I never questioned what they were doing, because it seemed so beautiful to me, it must have stemmed from the concealed hand of divine providence, a hand whose purpose had not become clear to me, and I was not to know about.

When cousin Hanna had to leave, she left the candleholders with us, as a present, I thought, but we never used them the same way we did with her being around, and I looked at them as something special…I almost heard her sing then…

◆   ◆   ◆

At the same time the white bread had appeared in the bakery one could also buy white flour, and occasionally Mama would bake very delicious bread on Fridays, for which she braided the dough in three layers on top of each other with the first braid being the widest and the third one the thinnest.

By then Mama would be called upon very often by the nearest hospital to donate blood, and then she received extra stamps for many eggs, milk and butter. She would put many eggs into the dough, that was probably what made the bread so tasty…much tastier than those white rolls.

When Mama made those awfully smelling latkes, it was around Christmas time, and we had been able to receive a package of small white candles. Mama would set them on the table in a half-circle, light one more every night and let them burn for a very little while.

I could not understand why she did that as I could not understand how she could cook latkes in cod liver oil.

Why did she waste all those candles and did not wait until one had burned down to light the next one? For the first time I did not agree with Mama's actions. They did not make sense to me, and I refused to try those latkes; I held my head out of the window instead, that made all the candles go out which, in turn, made Mama sad…But why did she not explain what was going on? Later, she told me, later, when you are old enough to get the meaning…she never ever told me, but she also never ever again cooked latkes in cod liver oil…

Years later, when there was no more rationing, she would cook latkes at different times in real oil, without any candles burning, and I remember those latkes to have become my favorite food. Mama would put them onto my plate right from the frying pan. And I would always eat so many that I had to lie down afterward.

We never used those two silver candleholders anymore, she kept them in a cabinet, only took them out once in a while to polish the silver…

But I kept these unanswered questions alive deep in my heart…

She would also teach me how to bake the braided bread, and called it only a braid.

◆   ◆   ◆

By next spring, after I just had turned eight, we had to go to school every day and stay there for several hours, one week in the morning the alternate week starting right after noon.

There were not enough classrooms available for so many pupils. We still received our daily soup at school at midday, and during break we would get two half slices of bread with cheese, we had never had before, and we even got a hot cup of broth.

There would also be care-packages from America with wonderful used clothes. I received a coat for the first time after the war, and did not need to wear the jacket and pants anymore that Mama had sewed by hand out of our heavy blanket. I knew she meant well and those things had kept me warm, but it was such an itchy material, that I was only too eager to get rid of this outfit and grateful to those nice people across the big ocean that had sent the coat and other things.

Otherwise the living situation had gotten worse, especially food distribution. Even with our stamps we could not buy what we needed. The black market was flourishing.

I took Mama's priceless photo camera to the open black market and received in exchange a small carton of water biscuits. The farmers had long ago quit taking anything for bartering; they now did their business on a larger scale. People were joking about them having to put one Oriental rug on top of the other in their pig stables because there was no room left in their houses for all those wares.

Mama had become friendly with Lotti's mother who was doing the laundry for the British soldiers and was a smoker.

So Mama got from her some soap flakes in exchange for cigarettes. No such thing like soap or bathroom tissue was being sold anywhere. But there was the newspaper!

I recall the day a former Polish forced labor worker asked Mama if she would knit a sweater for him. He only had some green yarn and a sailor's work sweater which Mama unraveled and knitted a striped marine blue and green sweater out of.

This man paid Mama with the most delicious things I have ever tasted: canned sausage, jelly, cheese and something, Mama had not had in years, real bean coffee. In addition to all that she could keep all the leftover yarn. She put it to good use, and I would have different outfits, gloves and shawls in either blue or green or mixed together…which, at that time, was not considered a right color combination…

The nice young man and Mama started to work together. He brought her coffee to sell for incredible high amounts, and for every pound she sold on the black market she would be rewarded with an eighth of a pound of coffee for herself. She could not sell coffee to her co-workers, because selling at black market prices was illegal.

But how could one survive without?

He always brought something for me, too—a piece of candy or some cookies, things I had not seen before.

The strangest food he ever gave me was an orange. It was the first orange I ever tried, and it tasted salty but was very juicy. I thought for the longest time that oranges had to taste that way, until I learned that this one had been in a box rescued from the bottom of the sea after a boat wreck.

◆　　　◆　　　◆

At that time we had to stay in elementary school until the end of sixth grade. Thereafter, one could move up to the higher school level, if one had past several tests. Every-one had to take English as first foreign language starting in fifth grade. So I finally had learned a little more than just a few words.

We did not have any paper to write on then, but Mama let me use her old diaries, cousin Hanna had saved for long, long years. I could not decipher the handwriting though; it was not in the Latin scripture that we were taught in. Since Mama had used up quite a few scribbling pads, only writing on one side of the pages, I would start them backwards and upside down, making me believe that I had an empty rough book in front of me.

If only I had known then what I know now, after trying to put some sense into the scribbling…so many things would have turned out quite differently…!

Some girls would bring brown wrapping paper to write on.

I used that only for my paintings…

Those three years I had spent in that school had been pretty tumultuous. The age difference between all of us was remarkable. No wonder that one not very nice old teacher shouted at us: *Wir sind hier nicht in einer Judenschule!* We are not in a Jew school! Whatever that meant, I did not know at that time. Yet, the not nice old teacher did not teach any longer!

When I entered girl's high school, *Maedchen Oberschule*, as the former *Lyceum* was now called, I was ten and the oldest girl in my class was already seventeen!

We entered high school at Quarta, i.e. seventh grade and had to take an additional foreign language, which was French in seventh, then Latin in eighth grade.

I loved to learn those languages. Our teachers were very old though and not always up to date. They had to study and get into those subjects just ahead of us which were also pertaining to the other subjects. Most of those teachers had already been retired and had to be reinstated. And teaching such a big crowd of so different ages must have been a terrible experience for them. I know the majority did not like to be part of the collegiums.

Although most of us were eager to learn and were trying to behave, some of us had to play jokes, maybe even cruel jokes on specific teachers.

We were educated in thirteen different subjects, and in future years we would even be taught in several more, we would have no way out of a single one!

♦   ♦   ♦

This transfer to a new school was coinciding with the *Waehrungsreform,* currency reform. That was the time when every one got a new start.

Forty *Deutsche Mark* per capita was all each and every person received; the *Reichsmark* was of no value anymore, the rationing was over with, and all of the sudden there were shelves full of food, delicacies I could have never imagined existing.

Every one was in awe, especially we children.

But again, there were only a few people who could buy all those goodies. I do not know where they got their additional money from, because Mama told me that every one's bank accounts had been frozen for the time being.

She thought that it would not take too long anymore until we would receive the money my Tate had saved for me. But now it would not be worth much since the money, the Reichsmark was devalued.

On the other hand you could buy a lot for that little money. Mama told me to look at the bright side: she would be paid in the new currency by the end of the month, our rent was very low, and soon we could get rid of our little stove-oven with its ugly oven pipe sticking through our live-in-kitchen's window, and we could replace the window panels' cardboard with glass. The central heat would be working again; so would gas, water and electricity.

And there were school supplies and books back in the stores again. Mama would buy me new pads and a real fountain pen, and I could do away with Mama's journals.

But it still would take several more years, until we could learn from newly edited school books.

And yet an other problem had to be addressed, a problem Mama and I had never talked about. Entering the new school meant to tell everything about your parents, their occupation, your place of birth and your religion.

I knew by then that my mama had been a nurse for many, many years, starting in the First World War until she got married to my father.

Now she was working at a public library as a librarian, and I was proud of her.

I would tell that my father had died when I was still a small child. He had died from the consequences of an injury he had suffered while fighting in the First World War. That was what Mama had told me when I wanted to know his cause of death.

But the part referring to my religion had never been discussed at home, and so the only thing I could do, when my new classroom teacher would ask that question, was shrug my shoulders, because I really did not know how to answer.

Each girl in my class was either Catholic or Protestant, there was none else. Mama told me, I should say as it was written in her identity card, which was *gottglaeubig*, meaning: believing in God. Later I learned that this word was only a make believe, it did not mean that the person who was *gottglaeubig*, was really believing in the One God, it was a Hitler invention that sounded good. I do not know why Mama told me to say just that. But I did, although then I still had to stay in class when religion was being taught to the Protestant group, which was the majority.

There it occurred to me that I did not know anything about Christianity. I was familiar with the Christmas Holiday, where some people were decorating a Christmas tree, put candles onto the branches and would light them all at the same time.

Mama never did that, she told me that we would rather use the wood for our oven if we were that lucky to get a tree. She also told me that Christmas meant for many people out there celebrating the birth of a baby, called Jesus, who was born around that time over nineteen hundred years ago. When I asked her who he was or what had become of him, she only mentioned that he was a prophet and a very good man, but there were many people who believed he was the son of God. He was the reason for Christianity.

Now I would get confused. I knew that there was only one God. But the other girls and the teacher wanted me to believe that there was a Trinity: God, the Father and his son, Jesus, and the Holy Spirit. I only could listen and had to keep my opinion to myself, but I could not stand that I was to participate in this class.

After Mama had gone to school and talked to my classroom teacher, I would be excused from taking that class. I was allowed to go together with girls from higher grades to be taught in philosophy, to even look at different religious beliefs, which I enjoyed very much, although some things were really hard to comprehend; yet, I especially liked what philosophy was all about: the aim for the real knowledge, for wisdom and the investigation of the truths and principles of being.

I never learned what Mama had told my teacher, who still treated me like her favorite student as she had done from the first day. So did most of the others. But some teachers treated me differently after that incident. They kept their distance and made me feel like an outsider.

I thought that this was just because I was so much younger than the other girls, and they were not used to answering difficult questions asked by a curious ten year old.

My friend, Lotti, did not treat me differently though, she told me that most people did not even know the meaning of Christmas, they just wanted to celebrate and get presents. At least that's how it was in her family.

After I had told my mama about this custom in Lotti's family, she would start to get us a small tree every year, but insisted that we only needed eight candles on our tree, which was all right with me.

I started reading about all those different religions, as we were being introduced to in philosophy class in an objective way. We were offered views and theories on profound questions in life and ethics. We learned about Indian and Chinese philosophy. We were taught to read about Voltaire and Rousseau as well as Espinoza and the old Greek philosophers like Plato and Socrates and many others.

Then there were those philosophers like Hegel, who caught my attention by secularizing religious starting points.

How proud was I then that my father had been a philosopher too! But what did he write about? Why did Mama not have his books, only a small poetry book, called *The Voice of the Earth*, which I had read over and over again without really understanding?

That was the time when I seriously wanted to know more about my father. But Mama would not explain, and I was saddened by her constant changing the subject following my inquiries.

I tried to investigate on my own; but there was nothing to start with. So, I had to be content with reading other philosopher's excerpts.

Every theory, however, did lead me back to my conviction that there was only one God, even though he might have had different names in different religions, or his existence totally denied as, for instance, Sartre and other atheistic philosophers did.

And I started to read about Jesus and Christianity. What I did not understand though, was why they were talking about Christianity as if

Jesus had invented it as a new religion. But nowhere could I find it written in the Bible that Jesus was a Christian. He was a Jew like all the other men of his time who were not Roman or Pagan. As it is said in the Gospel he was from the house of David. This means that he was a Jew.

And his disciples were also Jews. Maybe he just wanted to reform Judaism, and people later made him Christ? But do not Christus/Cristos mean "anointed"? Then who did anoint him? It could not have been GOD. GOD does not allow any one beside him!

What I read in the Bible was that the Jewish people were waiting for the Messiah to come, the Messiah, the deliverer! When Jesus was the Messiah why then did the people not know it and say that the Jews killed Jesus? Why should the Jews have killed one of their own? That did not make any sense to me. As I read it the Romans made the decision to crucify him.

Something else made me think that Christianity must be an invented religion, why are so many positive sayings and actions from the Old Testament now in the New Testament speeches and actions ascribed to Jesus?

But how could so many well educated people think differently than I? There must be something else about this man what I could not see!

◆   ◆   ◆

I did not know anything about as to where exactly we had lived in Vienna, Mama only referred sometimes to our house in Ottakring, and then she told me that I used to take a bath in the river Vienna near our house? I did not know where my father was born either, only that he had several siblings. But when I asked Mama to let me at least have information about our relatives in Vienna, my grandparents, uncles and aunts, she would only tell me that it was better for me not to ask any more of those questions, since she could not answer them.

Was that really true, how could that be? She must have kept contact with our families.

Then I realized that I would have known that, I was the one who picked up the mail that had fallen through the slit in the door, should there ever had been any. The only letters I remember Mama receiving were from Cousin Hanna or one of her sisters.

But when I wrote to Hanna, all the answers I would receive were echoing Mama's.

She did not know anything, was so sorry to not being able to tell me more...

I had to let it go.

I had now a lot of homework to do, and I loved to paint.

Besides reading, painting had become my favorite hobby. There was never time enough though, because I still had to do the daily chores at home and take care of the shopping list and the cooking.

When Mama came home at night she sometimes looked very tired, was barely able to eat out of fear that her stomach would be upset afterward.

Finally she consulted a doctor, who would diagnose stomach ulcers that had to be surgically removed. She had to stay in the hospital for quite some time while I was home alone with Lora even during night time. But I was not scared to be alone, only scared that something might happen to my mama.

And I still had those nightmares hearing the sirens going off, the bombs falling, and people trampling each other to death. Sometimes they were killing my Tate...and I ran away!

Another thing that scared me all my life since the war, were real big thunderstorms...they are even now, almost fifty years later, a terrible reminder...

I was now about twelve years old and could handle things independently. I visited with my mama every day.

The hospital was close by, but it always made me sad to look into my mama's face which would show her pain and her age. She was fifty-four by then, about the same age my father was when I was born. That much knowledge I had been able to coerce out of her.

She still was pretty with her black curly hair I always wished I would have too! Especially when the other children were saying bad things about red heads. They even had a rhyme in German: *Rote Haare, Sommersprossen, sind des Teufels Volksgenossen*! Which means, loosely translated: red haired with freckles are the devil's companions. But Mama made me feel better about my long reddish curls when she would tell me that I was her best memory of my Tate especially with how my hair looked.

And I had just learned in biology class the law of Mendel…black was always the dominant color…!

At school things started to get a little more to normal.

We still had to take turns when class started, one week mornings, the next afternoons. But we had new teachers coming in, younger teachers, mostly women, who were student-teachers. They brought a wave of fresh air with them that really cleaned our old fashioned school atmosphere.

The regiment was yet kept strictly, but one could hear a lot of laughter throughout that old war-shattered building, where half a wing was off limits until it would be restored.

Mama was back to work again, though she seemed to be weak and tired, but did not admit it.

She still enjoyed reading and knitting at the same time, one of the things I would take after her in. She had shown me how to knit when I was four, at the same time when she had taught me all the other important things, as she called it. She always told me the being educated was the most important issue, something that no one could take away from me. And I loved to learn.

All those years ago it was very hard to get hold of any yarn, but somehow Mama had always managed…

Mama would even now bring the books from the library, and I always hated it when they had to be returned; I wanted to own those books, to read them whenever I felt like it, and every so often be able to make notes on some especially interesting subjects. It was a very intimate relationship I kept with some of those books…but to own them, was out of the question.

We needed so many other things, and Mama's salary was not very big.

Besides, she let me spend enough money on painting supplies, not on paper though; I would still use the brown wrapping paper for larger works.

Mama did not have a sewing machine. She did all the sewing by hand, created the most beautiful dresses for my first theater visit and other festivities.

She let me start again taking ballet classes which had been interrupted during war time. I did not remember to have taken ballet lessons in Vienna, but my body and feet did.

There were so many things I wanted to do, that did not even cost money. If there had only been more time!

School-breaks were always too short; although we had a long six weeks break during summer. But now we wanted to enjoy summers on the beach.

Hamburg is surrounded by water, and it never took long to find a way to take a swim and bask in the sun, I did not remember shining at all during war time. Neither did I remember to have heard the chirping and singing of birds during that time.

During the war about sixty per cent of the city's facilities were destroyed, and fifty-five thousand people were killed in Hamburg.

By now most of those ruins were either torn down totally and new houses rebuilt instead, or some areas were transformed into green spaces, little parks with trees, bushes and flowers, like new life was rising out of the ashes.

And many larger buildings arose that did not look as pretty as the old ones before the war but were serving their purpose. With so many refugees coming from the East, it was mandatory to find housing for them fast.

It took almost twenty years though to reconstruct the city.

Lotti, some other friends and I were always taking advantage of those sunny days. One time we dared to skip a two hour class in sports to go to the water.

Did we ever get a reason to regret this impulsive treat! We would get lines of imposition we were really not happy about and had to promise to never ever again break any school rules…

…until I realized that Lotti and some of our other girlfriends had found legitimate excuses to stay away from school: they had met some boys who did not take school seriously.

And I was being left out!

Mama again had to comfort me, this time it was different though, this time it really was the age difference; nothing else!

◆   ◆   ◆

What made me very upset at school was the fact that history as a subject was not being taught correctly. No teacher ever dared to talk about the most recent history, about the atrocities the Nazis did in the concentration camps and the Holocaust.

Not even the war was being mentioned, let alone the word Nazi!

We started out with ancient history and ended with Bismarck. That means that German history ended 1900. No first world war, no depression, or inflation, nothing else all the way through *Abitur* which was the school-leaving exam and university entrance qualification.

All I got to know about those terrible real history lessons I learned later in university.

While all my other teachers always expected me to become a philosopher or an other scientist, my art teacher wanted me to study art and become a painter. And I felt the same way; I wanted to become an artist, for to me art was means of communication, aiming to replace words. I was able to paint what I never could have expressed otherwise.

But my mama did not agree with my choice of a future profession.

We have had a lot of disagreements in the last year.

When I was sixteen Mama had to retire because of her deteriorating health, and now would become a stay at home mom. She would start to tell me every day what to do and not to do, like she had just become a mother.

Without acknowledging that I had been on my own for nine years now, she tried to make up for all the time lost to her as a mother. That was something that did not work, however. You can not turn back the clock, not bring back time you did not have to spend when you needed it. Time waits for no one.

Adding to my misery was the accidental death of Lora, my best friend and trusted companion. Since she was unable to fly she was always hobbleling on her somehow crippled feet, sometimes trying to hop which looked quite funny, and making complaining noises when she had to get from one place to the other. One day she must have miscalculated the height of her cage, made a wrong step fell down to the floor and broke her neck. I was so devastated. I cried for her, could not imagine life without my sweet Lora. Yet, I had to face the fact and bury her. All her songs she sang in her hoarse voice were played back inside me; all her funny talks she had made over the years were recounted; I started missing her immediately.

It probably sounds childish to grieve so much over a bird. But she was so much more to me!

◆   ◆   ◆

Mama insisted on my changing the choice I made for my future. I should go to medical school and could still paint as a hobby, maybe even take classes in art, but first I had to have a real job!

I enrolled in Hamburg University to become a physician when I was seventeen, underage to get my own way.

All the other students were so much older; several had been POWs for some years after serving in the army right out of school.

Those were the ones who would tell all of us who had been dumbfounded, what really had happened during the Nazi regime. They told us about the *Endloesung der Judenfrage*, the finalization of the persecution of the Jews. It was horrible! No human being could have been involved in those atrocious crimes!

I could not believe what I was hearing. How could those terrible, extremely shocking brutal acts been committed without the people knowing? Or did they know?

Who did? Did Mama know? Did the world around us know? Why did other countries not interfere? Was that what the war was all about?

And the main question: why did God let such cruelties happen? WHERE WAS God? Was there a God? Did God sleep?

So many questions. Where could I find an answer?

I did not tell Mama this time, I confronted her, and she cried, cried…for a long time. The first time I saw her cry!

She knew, she told me later, not to the real extend until after the war; it was such a Tohuvabohu at that time, but she knew, had heard about it on her radio and had to keep quiet, like everybody who knew, less you wanted to risk your own life and end up in a concentration camp too. Then she again wanted me to stop asking questions that became personal.

I did not understand her attitude at that time. The war was long over, I told her. All those millions of innocent people were dead, but they could not be forgotten, could they?

She nodded wearily, speechless at the same time, then, after a long while of silence she uttered only a few words: *But the hate for the Jewish people is not gone with the war.*

Was that true? How did she know?

I did not receive an answer this time either.

Why did she not answer my questions that were personal? Was she Jewish and I too? But how was it possible that nobody had come after us? Was that the reason I had this strange feeling about Christianity, because I knew in my heart that I was not one of them?

I was tormented by all those unanswered questions, and on the other hand somehow at peace with my inner self, I could not explain why.

But Mama would not give any hint, even when I straight out told her what had come to my mind…she would never tell me…and I did not have a clue as to how to find out more, or anything at all for that matter.

I had to let go again and go on with my studies.

◆   ◆   ◆

The only thing during my medical studies that really made me sick to my stomach was the first time I had to pay a visit to the anatomy department in the basement of the university.

Later I got used to that too and had to work down there for quite some time as all the other students did.

There were only low fees to be paid per semester, books could be rented from the library of the university, and otherwise education was almost for free if you qualified.

◆   ◆   ◆

Being always depending on my mother to pay for things I would like to buy, made me feel too miserable, knowing that she did not allow herself anything. This feeling of guilt would force me to look for a job at a time I did not have to attend important lectures at university. However, there was nothing available during daytime.

All my friends from school who did not want to study further, and tried to get an apprenticeship in any field had problems finding a place.

Lotti finally served her apprenticeship with an attorney although she had rather gone into an architectural office. She at least was earning some money while I had only been able to sell a few of my paintings, to write some small articles for a local newspaper that paid only ten *Pfennig* per line.

Money was tight everywhere. People in general wanted to start living again and every one wanted to be a part of the reconstruction of a country where almost nothing was remaining when the war had ended eleven years ago.

Finally I took a job as a waitress in a piano bar for some hours at night.

Mama would not approve of my decision. Somehow I could convince her though, but only on condition that she would take me there every night I had to work. Her worry was somehow degrading. I was not a little girl anymore! But if this was the only way I could make a few marks, so be it!

◆   ◆   ◆

There were several other students working in the bar. One girl studied chemistry; an other one was attending the music conservatory to become an opera singer. Although we would earn only eight Deutschmarks per night, it was a lot at that time. We did not get any tips though. Most customers were foreigners, business men who could not speak German or only a little.

I think that was the first reason the boss had hired us, because we were able to communicate with those men. They were always nicely dressed, always wearing a necktie, they would not have been allowed into the bar without.

◆   ◆   ◆

There were also a few German customers who would become regulars.

None of them was young I noticed. They probably could not have afforded those high priced cocktails.

What I thought to be coincidental was that one guest in particular was there every night I was working. He never came alone, every time he had some other gentleman in tow.

One night he would bring with him an Italian friend and after giving his order, he asked me several questions and seemed very interested in my studies.

Since I was at work I could not risk talking to him any longer. He asked me if he and his friend could invite me to do some sightseeing together on the upcoming Sunday. I could bring a friend.

I had to think it over and talked with Gerti, the chemistry student with whom I had become friends in the meantime.

She agreed to go with me and we arranged to be picked up at my place.

I did not think of this being a date. This man could have easily been my father, age-wise, I mean. His Italian friend seemed much younger though, and I contemplated that they just wanted some company during their sightseeing tour.

When I told my mother about this encounter she started to give a long sermon about female behavior and about men in general.

She should have given that talk years ago, but probably did not know how and when the time was right. This time was definitely not the right one. She made me feel like a little girl again, and I was already in my fourth semester of medical school!

I knew how to handle men. I was surrounded by lots of them in the university. We even had partied together, went dancing, and I had gone to the movies with some of them. But we always were in a group, no one on one relationship there that I know of. The male students were as eager as we females were, to get through all those quite difficult courses.

In retrospect it comes to mind that we all were far too serious, too much focused on our future and not enjoying the present.

We were deprived of our childhood, never knew how to simply have fun, and now we did not know how we should act as young adults.

I was only eighteen years old but it sometimes felt as if I had already collected the experience of a full lifetime. While I had incorporated my mother's sorrows and her silence as part of my being, the other part, however, was unconsciously seeking for something imaginary, some kind of wholeness for there was a void that could not be filled.

◆   ◆   ◆

Sunday arrived. Gerti came early. We should be picked up by one in the afternoon.

Mama's long lecture did not leave a big impression. I knew by now that she would never change her always adverse, almost hostile attitude against any stranger who might be intruding our privacy.

What made the whole endeavor even more difficult was that I did not know the names of those two gentlemen, who arrived punctually.

My mother opened the door which relieved me of introducing them. The German was the first to enter and with a likeable smile bowed and stated his name as Dr. Hans Neumann, and then with an inviting gesture he made the introduction of his Italian friend, Dr. Enrico Avieri.

This friend Enrico was speaking a very broken German which loosened up those first awkward moments and made all of us laugh a little, kind of relieved and embarrassed at the same time.

We only made some small talk and, without any further rules of conduct, my mother would send us on our way.

I guess she was a little intimidated by those two doctors.—

Hans Neumann had a big car waiting in front of our apartment building. I did not know much about cars at that time, but learned that it was an Opel Kapitaen that was very comfortable, in contrast to my self-consciousness.

I would be seated next to the driver and Gerti sat in the back with Enrico. The conversation started slowly on the female part. Both of us felt somewhat misplaced in this unfamiliar environment with those so obviously experienced, well read and globetrotting males.

Again it was Enrico's little knowledge of the German language that saved us from this afternoon to become a total disaster.

We would park the car somewhere downtown, walk to a coffee shop and be invited to a wonderful piece of cake and coffee.

My mother had introduced me to coffee after I had turned sixteen, and I remember not liking it at all at the beginning. Later, during all our exams I was happy this dark liquid was available. It made it much easier to stay up late and study. But, I also had started a very bad habit as my mother called it, I had begun smoking cigarettes.

I told her that everybody did it, which was not a good argument I have to acknowledge, but the only one that came to mind when Mama confronted me.—

After we had enjoyed our cake and gratefully declined a second helping, it was no surprise for any of us when the two men asked if we would mind them smoking. We were only too keen to follow our desire to do the same. While Gerti and I joined Enrico who would pass his pack of cigarettes around, Hans took one of those small dark cigars out of a tiny metal case, then he rose to offer us fire.

Good manners could not be denied!

After a while we all would become more relaxed in our conversation and my answers to Hans's questions came easily.

As we had finished our coffee and Hans had taken care of the bill, we went for a stroll around the Alster and pretended to do window shopping.

And there we went two by two, Enrico and Gerti and Hans and I.

It seemed like it was being planned that way, but no one had suggested it. It came naturally.

It was amazing how much this older man and I had in common, not only was he a physician and a lecturer at the university, he also was well educated and informed in all the other topics I was interested in.

And he was a very good listener. We talked mostly about medical issues. In the meantime I had decided to become a pediatrician and was telling him about that, also that I had originally wanted to study art, but upon my mother's request was now in med school.

I tried to make him understand that I had not the feeling of being forced into studying medicine, I even convinced myself by saying it out loud that I now loved to have made that choice.

I was still painting as often as possible but unable to take night classes because I wanted to earn at least my own spending money.

We did not talk about anything in regard of other private matters though. Just exchanging thoughts and ideas about improving the curriculum, getting students more interested in the theoretic and ways of decreasing population in the laboratories.

I was only one semester short of the *Physikum*, which is the preliminary examination in medicine. Afterwards I would be working in all different sections and departments at the university hospital.

He knew all my professors which to me was a very weird, odd feeling, so uncanny that I did not know how to respond to this revelation. Was he trying me, did he want to know what I as a student was thinking of his colleagues, just checking for whatever purpose and then tell on me? But as I looked up into his gentle open face, dominated by gray friendly eyes, I could only dismiss those thoughts. He really was interested in my opinion about their teaching attitude and not about to judge me on that account.

Being so animated by his genuine curiosity I only heard Gerti and Enrico laughing in a distance.

There was not much sightseeing after all, which led me to the conclusion that this terminology was only meant as an excuse to welcome their invitation.

This interpretation somehow did puzzle me. Why haven't they only asked us out? Would I have accepted that, would Gerti have? I did not know the answer and was not about to find out. Why did I always have to investigate the motivation for other people's actions? Why not just enjoy the moment?

After asking us if we would care for having dinner together which we turned down appreciatively, they would drive us back to my place early in the evening, but not without requesting to exchange phone numbers.

Mama seemed to be pleased that we came home within a timely manner and did not bring those gentlemen with us.

Shortly thereafter Gerti left. She had an early course she had to attend, and so did I.

My mother did not make any notion about this afternoon's event and I left this issue alone.

◆   ◆   ◆

The next time I was working, Hans and his friend were there again. Had it only been two days ago that we were sitting in the coffee shop on our *sight seeing* tour?

Hans did not behave any differently than he had before our outing, he probably did not want anyone to know. Maybe he would not even have acknowledged it in public.

It did not mean anything to him. It was just what I assumed to begin with: they only wanted some company on their *tour*. But what tour? It definitely was not a sight seeing tour.

Why ponder, Liva? It was only a nice gesture, wasn't it?

As Gerti told me during a bathroom break, Enrico was not mentioning the meeting to her either. Still, I could not figure out why they would invite us in the first place.

They did not stay very long this time, had only a couple of drinks and left.

After work Gerti and I usually walked together to the next city railroad which took us into different directions.

To our surprise, we found Enrico, Hans and his car waiting to take us home.

They just did not want us to use the city railroad but give us a ride instead. So Hans said. And so they did.

We first drove to Gerti's place which was the nearest. Enrico walked her to the door of her apartment complex, and then they took me home. We did not talk much during the ride, I was tired as usual after work, and Hans only took my hand, thanked me for the pleasure to let him take me home, waited until I had turned the house key, then said good night, and was back in his car, before I even had the opportunity to utter a thank you!

…Strange, I thought, but pleasant. Did that mean I did not know men after all?

◆   ◆   ◆

I remember to have slept wonderfully that night.

The next day I received a call from Hans, asking me if I would like to go out for dinner with him. After telling him that I still needed my mother's permission, he assured me that he would take care of that.

We set a date when I did not have to work, and he came to ask my mother for approval.

Was he ever in for a questioning! Mama wanted to know everything about him before she reluctantly agreed to let me go out with him! I felt so embarrassed. It made me blush, I was mortified. But Hans did not seem to mind. He answered every question in a humble manner.

We learned that he was in his early forties, had gone through a divorce two years ago after a fourteen year marriage to a once before divorced woman, eight years his senior, and no, there were no children.

And that he was a lecturer at the medical faculty of the university. He even told us that growing up a Catholic he was supposed to become a priest and was being taught by Jesuits in a boarding school to be a missionary in Brazil.

But he knew that was not his calling and that he had to run away from boarding school one year prior to his graduation in order to become a doctor.

His father had been missing in action in W.W.I, when he was only one year old.

Later, when he was about seven, his mother was remarried to a man who could not tolerate his passion for reading and studying. That's when his uncles took him to his grandparent's farm where he was raised until he had to attend boarding school.

How could he pursue his plans to become a physician when he did not have the qualification certificate to enter medical school? Mama went too far with her inquisition!

It was not that he was about to marry me!

Why did she need to know everything? I was ashamed, but there was nothing I could do to avoid further humiliating interrogations. Hans did not loose his composure and remained calm by answering every single question.

He stated that he had later taken an aptitude test, called *Begabtenpruefung*, especially designed for gifted students, one of Hitler's inventions. Hans was somewhat hesitant when talking about that, because now he had to admit that he owed his career in some way to this invention and consequently to Hitler.

Hence I was not in the least surprised when the next question was, if he had been a member of the Nazi party. He had to acknowledge that too, adding that he had been forced to become a *Jungstahlhelm*, otherwise he would have never been allowed to study medicine.

If Mama had problems swallowing this confession, she sure did not show it, and we were released, free to go out.

Now it was up to me to do some damage control. I started apologizing for my mother's bluntness and offensive investigation. Hans would stop me right there, telling me that he had been totally understanding, in fact, he pretended to be somehow jealous that my mother was so protective of me.

He did not have that support from his mother while growing up. She did not even know where he went after leaving boarding school;

neither did she make an attempt to find out. During that time they had not heard from each other for many years.

Everything he had accomplished this far he had done on his own, working at the university with students from foreign countries, doing regular office work there and tutoring on evenings to pay his tuition. Later his future mother in law had taken care of him financially and given him moral support.

Fortunately she did not have to watch her daughter become an alcoholic after they had been married for about ten years. His wife could not understand his ambition to become a professor at university. She wanted him to work in his private practice instead of teaching students.

During the war he had to serve as a surgeon in the army where part of it at that time had been stationed in Denmark.

Now we had a lot to talk about during our first real date.

◆   ◆   ◆

The dinner was delicious; I cannot remember what we ate, though. I was still contemplating as to why he had taken interest in me, and finally, I dared to ask him about that.

And, to my amazement, he actually answered that I was the woman he had always dreamed about, that he fell in love with me the first time he had laid eyes on me, that's why he had to come back every night I worked.

He had observed my every move, my attitude with other customers, and he had come to the conclusion that I would be the only one he would want to be willing to spend the rest of his life with…if I would agree to become his wife…

I could not believe what I was hearing! He was a grown man with a past, and I was still a teen-ager who did not yet know what falling in love meant! Sure, I liked him, liked his company, and liked the way he was talking, smiling at me.

But marriage was one thing that had never entered my mind. I did not want to get married for a long time. I wanted to have a career, to become a pediatrician and to have time to still do my artwork.

I tried to explain this to him, to be honest about my feelings for him, that I liked him very much, but did not love him, whatever that meant in my humble opinion.

I could as well have spoken to the wind! He had an explication for everything: when I only wanted to reason, he defined and illustrated how wonderful it would be working together, traveling together and, yes, I should have my career, but without the need to work for my own spending money. And if I really liked him, then I would definitely come to love him eventually. He could open a whole new world for me…

What was I getting into? What would my mother say? Was this a genuine proposal? I did not know how to respond.

He painted our future in so many beautiful ways, that I finally agreed to think about it.

Hans wanted my reply as soon as possible, though. After I should have given him the answer he was hoping for, he would formally ask my mother for my hand in marriage.

My head was spinning. Somehow it all sounded so enticing! Was I dreaming? Everything he had told me made sense in a total different way as I had planned my future, but it made sense.

I was still lost in my own thoughts, had not spoken a word during our ride home, when Hans stopped the car in front of my apartment building. Opening my car door, he looked worried and serious, but wanted me to assure him that there was hope. I smiled at him, gave him a peck on his cheek and ran inside.

When I told Mama the whole amazing story she was not at all surprised. That's what she had expected. That's why she had questioned him so thoroughly.

Her only real argument against marriage was that he was too old for me; he was closer to her age than mine. I knew that, why did she have to point it out?

But Tate was also much older than she, I tried to bicker. It was a lame protest, though; Tate was only twelve years her senior, not almost twenty-five!

At least he was not Catholic anymore which seemed to have found Mama's approval. How would she know that? Neither she nor I had asked him about his religious beliefs. Mama explained to me that he had been divorced, moreover had married a divorcee, which in itself was a sin. Those facts automatically get Catholics excommunicated.

I probably had not paid attention to those facts if they had come up in philosophy class back in school.

When I finally asked my mother what answer I should give him, she only looked me in the eyes and told me that this was my decision, mine alone. I should know the pros and cons by now. I was not a child anymore.

Thanks, mama, for reminding me! I was about to say. But this time she was right to throw this adverse fact into my face. I was a grown woman of eighteen and could make my own decision!

Next day I called Hans and told him that I would be willing to accept his proposal.

◆   ◆   ◆

We got engaged soon thereafter.

Before we got married I visited his nice little country home in the suburbs of Hamburg. It was a beautiful big lot with a small but comfortable house. Adjacent he had his practice where he used to treat patients only on days he did not have to teach at the university.

Hans already had lots of blueprints for renovating and adding on to the house.

There was a housekeeper, an older lady who lived in a small room next to the kitchen. Several other people were roaming around, and it took me some time to get to know who they were and what kind of position they were holding.

Two little Scotch terriers were part of the family and Frau Witt, the housekeeper, was spoiling them.

◆   ◆   ◆

The wedding took place in a private setting. Since it was only a civil ceremony being held in the registry office, we only needed two witnesses, my mother and Enrico. Gerti had come too, so did some other friends of ours.

Afterwards, Hans had arranged for a luscious dinner in one of the city's fanciest hotels. We were all having a good time. What I did not understand was the fact that there was no dancing.

I had never attended a wedding before, but still asked Hans later about the usual customs. His excuse was that he forgot to ask me about this form of amusement, rather sheepishly admitting that he could not dance. And I loved to dance! I told him that we had to do something about it.

There was no such thing as *cannot dance*. He just had to learn it. He promised that this would be the first thing he was willing to try for my sake.

◆   ◆   ◆

We spent our honeymoon in Venice, Italy. But the whole car ride toward our destination was already such a wonderful experience for me.

We drove down near the Rhine river, stayed in a beautiful little hotel in the Alps, took the car by train through the St. Gotthard tunnel, made a stop at Locarno, visited Zurich, and finally got to Venice, where we would stay for ten days in the most luxurious hotel near St. Marco.

Really, a whole new world had been opened to me!

We were having so much fun listening to the gondolier singing in his wonderful Italian while maneuvering his gondola through the romantic canals, every so often pointing out to us famous buildings of long gone famous people.

We walked through all those small cobblestone alleys, fed the pigeons of St. Marco and took a boat-ride to the famous Murano, where Hans bought everything I would take a closer look at. He really spoiled me like a princess, and that's how he called me: his little golden-haired princess.

Hans was the gentlest generous man a girl could have asked for. He was always calm and answered whatever question came up, never ceasing to amaze me with his unlimited knowledge and patience.

◆   ◆   ◆

I got to know my husband and I learned that there was yet an other side I had just discovered: he was in a way very self-conscious, insecure pertaining to all things associated with society.

Besides his scientific knowledge I had the feeling he felt lost, he did not know anything about music, classical or contemporary, nothing about art, about theater or literature. He used to read constantly, but only medical or other scientific journals. He did not remember to have ever read a novel at all.

That's where his inability of dancing fit into.

He asked me if I would be willing to teach him, familiarize him with all those social activities.

He did not volunteer the facts to me that his first wife had made him believe that he was not cut out for life in public; he had been raised on a farm, right? Never been educated for social life.

She must have persuaded him of this that it became a permanent imprint in his memory, not easily to be erased. And he had trusted her fully!

How could that have happened? How could a person convince another human being to only be worthy in working as a physician and totally inadequate in almost any other way of life?

I was not willing to fathom that, and I told him so. Hans was admitting then that they had never attended any university outings, cultural events or gatherings, not even parties together because of that, and he was still hesitant when I told him he simply had to let go of those futile thoughts.

He could do and be anything he wanted to if he only would set his mind to it and overcome his shyness.

But I noticed how deeply rooted his fear of failure was!

Only in the last two and a half years he had seen that there was life after work!

And now he had found me and, together we would conquer all those obstacles!

I loved him for that. For his faith in me and his confidence that together we could beat all the odds.

◆   ◆   ◆

We purchased a condominium near the university and I learned how to drive. I sometimes still thought I was dreaming sitting behind the wheel, for only a few months ago I was saving for a bicycle!

The addition to the country home was finished by now and during the weekends we enjoyed staying there.

I had started studying again after our long honeymoon break and attended every course I had to until our first son arrived.

Hans was overjoyed when he first learned that I was pregnant, and now he could not take his eyes off this little bundle of joy.

Mama was very proud to hold her little grandson and visited me every day while I was in university hospital. My room was a sea of flowers. Hans had introduced me with pride to all his colleagues as soon as we had come back from our tour through Italy.

He wanted to show me that his intentions of becoming more outgoing and sociable were genuine.

Every one was very nice to me, and now I had my new friends visiting me in the maternity ward and showering me with gifts.

I had already started to work on my dissertation and had taken all my paperwork with me to the hospital. However, all this traffic there kept me from writing anything.

◆   ◆   ◆

I finally would meet Hans' mother who was very proud that her late husband's name now would be passed on to the next generation. She was very tall and had an impressive stature. By comparison, though, she looked far older than my mama, who was only a few years younger than she.

My mother in law stayed only a short time. I never really got to know her, because a year thereafter she suddenly passed away.

◆   ◆   ◆

The first few weeks after Rafael's birth I would stay home with him. Rafael was my mama's suggestion, for one of her ancestors had been named so, and she really wanted this name to live on. It was all right with Hans.

After four weeks one of our secretaries would bring the baby to the university at feeding time and two of the many assistants at home would take turns to tending to his every need. My mother was supervising all those activities. But this was not a long term solution.

One day my mother would announce that she had found the perfect protector for our child, Cousin Hanna! I did not know how she did it, but she would convince Hanna that she was the only one able to take care of our child.

So, Hanna first became Rafael's nanny, but soon took over the whole housekeeping business. Everything but cleaning was now her responsibility. We had to let go the old housekeeper of Hans' time as a bachelor.

Hanna sure had not changed much since I had to say good-bye to her when I was seven. Just a little older and chubbier. And she did not address my mother as Yentl or Yenta anymore as I remembered her doing back than.

I was overcome with joy to just see her again and really hoped she would start talking and singing with Mama as she used to when I was a child. When I asked her about that, she became very sincere while telling me that this would not be appropriate, especially in this environment where low language definitely was out of line.

All my persuasion could not change her mind, even after I had explained that Hans had been reared in rural Westphalia, where the spoken dialect was a very strange one, not at all High German, she insisted on never ever to ask her again and not to mention that special east Prussian to my husband. Neither should I talk about our old traditions we used to hold on to.

I was disappointed and felt somehow betrayed because she did not give a real explanation for her refusal. Also, I found it very odd that she would never address Hans as a family member. She was my first cousin, wasn't she? She should have called him by his first name, right, and not always refer to him as *Herr Professor*?!

Mama told me to just forget about it. The main issue at hand was that she was a wonderful nanny and a very good cook and that Hans was very fond of her. That was true in every way. He would mention those facts by thanking her after each meal she had prepared so deliciously.

And she was the best nanny for our little son he assured her.

Now I knew that my child was well taken care of and I could put all my energy into my studies.

◆   ◆   ◆

I had abandoned my first choice for my dissertation; it just would not work out as I wanted it to. I approached my adviser to talk to him about a new research I was eager to start. I wanted to find the correlation between the growth of the metacarpal bones and the development of the roots of deciduous teeth in children. I received his approval and started with my exploration of this interesting subject matter.

Fortunate for me was that I had access to the X-ray equipment in Hans' practice. However, as soon as I noticed being pregnant again I had to let our assistants take the shots.

When our second son was born I had already accumulated quite a few challenging data that I could work with while in the hospital.

A few weeks prior to Timothy's arrival we had found a maid who would be helping Hanna with whatever chores needed to be done. She got her own room and was called a house daughter.

As soon as I wanted to go to the university again, Hans hired a nanny right out of nanny school who was only to care for the newborn and who, too, would live in our house. Hanna was still in charge with everything and had especially fallen in love with the new baby.

Again, I could not finish my studies. This time it was a daughter, a beautiful little redheaded lady whom we would name Cornelia, but call Nele.

Now we had three children in a row, and I wanted to finish my medical exams and write my dissertation.

◆   ◆   ◆

Mama was enjoying her status as a grandmother, was always welcome to stay with us, but she kept her apartment in the city and came only for birthdays or when Hans and I were on vacation.

I guess that she and Hanna were rejoicing in reliving old times and traditions while we were gone.—

In Mama's opinion we now had enough children anyway.

I had finished my first doctoral exams, was now a general practitioner and had received my degree.

This achievement had come with a high price tag: time, I was not able to spend with my babies. When I left in the morning, they were still asleep, and when I finally would be home, they were already asleep.

Over the weekends I managed somehow to make good for the lost time; but now there were so many social events we had to attend!

I eventually had kept my promise to teach Hans social skills. He even had taken dancing lessons with me and some other couples who were like Hans charter members of our local Lions' Club.

At first he did not want to join this organization, but I could convince him that he had to be around people of all different backgrounds and professions.

And he started to like it. I knew he was a wonderful speaker at the university as well as a beloved teacher. Now he had to overcome his reservations and show his ability to talk freely about different issues. He did it as well as I expected.

He started telling stories to the kids at nighttime, which was especially appreciated by Rafael.

Sometimes trying to get around it, Hans would offer a choice between watching TV and story. Rafael always voted for a story and his two little siblings joined forces, and with much laughter, Daddy had to give in.

But I still wanted to become a pediatrician, which, again, would keep me away from my family for several more years!

Hans would try in a very subtle way to talk me out of this sacrifice. I should become a stay at home mom, and with Nele being almost two, he was implying that we needed an other baby.

That was not necessarily identical with my idea of spending my future, but what did I have to complain about?

At least I would be able to paint, something I did not have much time for during the last five years. Hans had let someone construct a studio for me, with an adjacent sewing room next to the children's playroom.

And, as he would put it, I did not need to give up on my dream to work as a pediatrician, there would be enough work for me treating our own children. I just could keep up with the current pediatric guidelines by reading my way through on my own.

Hans made it sound like it was not an important issue, but to me it was a big decision to give up on going further in my studies.

What have I been working for so hard for so many years when I should not ever be having a career as a doctor?

I definitely did not want to practice as a general practitioner. My husband also did not want me to; he only said that this would always be a possibility to fall back on when the kids were grown. When would that be, wasn't he just talking about us having an other baby?

◆   ◆   ◆

There were so many things we did not talk about. It was as if some subjects had become taboo. It was only a gut feeling at the beginning, but I knew in my heart that I could trust my feelings, that they were mostly on the mark.

Here is where the age difference is coming into play, I figured. We came from different generations, and nothing could change that. I knew he loved me with all his being; he had assured me of that in many ways. And I loved him for loving me. But did I now owe him my life?

Why did he never answer my questions about his participation during the Nazi regime? Why did he insist on not having known anything of those atrocities that were being done?

He just had told me once that he had done something what would have incriminated him if any one knew: in order to do a close friend a favor, he had after the war the SS-tattoo surgically removed from his friend's arm! How could he have done that?

When we were having get-to-gethers with Lions friends from other countries, like Denmark and Sweden, at the beginning it occurred quite often that the issue of information, of awareness during the war had come up.

But it was not only Hans who was ignorant, all the German friends attempted to affirm our guests that they had not known a thing! How could they not have known, when my mother had admitted it?

This was very troublesome to me; to me it seemed to be just an accepted truth. I kept my doubts to myself, however!

Hans wanted to sell the condo near the university and tried to convince me to make the right decision by presenting me with my own car, a Mercedes convertible.

I gave in, and a year later we had a second little girl, named her Simone, and this time I could really enjoy the baby from the beginning all the way until the next one would arrive...

One night in November after Simone's birth, Mama called me to give me the terrible news about President Kennedy's assassination. She was in tears.

◆   ◆   ◆

The following January she was unable to come to celebrate Nele's birthday...and a few days later, her doctor called late at night, to tell us that my mama had passed away!

I did not want to believe it! I knew that she had suffered from angina pectoris and was taking Digitalis...

I never had a chance to tell her good-bye and that I loved her! It could not be true that I should not be able to talk to her any more. It could not be true! I did not want it to be true!

But it was a sad reality.

Now we did not know as to how she wanted to be buried. There was no will. Hanna was of no help there, either.

Hans would ask a friend from the Lions club, who too, was born in East Prussia and who was a retired minister, to take care of the funeral.

I remember everything just with a veil in front of my eyes. I must have been sleepwalking the whole time. Hans took care of all the formalities and brought most of my mama's possessions to our home.

I tried to pray as I had done as a child, sometimes guided by Mama or Hanna. But I had forgotten the prayers we had said together. Now I could only pray to God in my own words. My thoughts turned to all those wonderful moments we shared during our time together, even when they were the hardest!

I had always felt close to God, had developed kind of a personal relationship to Him. I told Him when I doubted Him, when I could not understand why things happened the way they did. God was the only one I could tell all my worries and I had the feeling, He was listening...

Yet, I did not have time to grieve, let alone go through Mama's things, because just a year later, we had an other daughter.

Alexandra was being followed by Tobias and finally Vita.

Now I had four kids under four years of age and three older ones. Not much older, though...

◆   ◆   ◆

We had hired a cook and some more help for Hanna, who really had changed after my mother's death.

In the meantime we had made quite a few additions to the house, and Hanna had her own apartment in a small guesthouse in the back of our lot. She was now overseeing all the in—home employees, would even sit with all of us at the dinner table which she refused to do as long as she was in charge with the cooking.

We always had our main meal at nighttime when Hans would be home from his work at the institute. He would not practice at our home anymore, only at the university where he had several attendants, assistants and secretaries.

My first maid was now married for some years to a soldier, but she came daily to do the laundry and always brought her three children with her.

The older kids also had their friends over, and it was no surprise to our nannies when people asked if this was a Kindergarten...

I enjoyed sewing and knitting clothes for the children and getting away from the crowd by painting in my studio.

◆　　◆　　◆

I never had given up on finding out more about my relatives on both sides. Hanna, though, still did not tell much, only that there had been several children in our grandparents' family. She just did not know what had happened to them, after her parents had gone to the Rhineland from East Prussia. Had lost contact. Sure, she had known our grandparents when they all had lived in the east, and that grandfather Zayde was a very handsome man with long black curls.

However, nobody had a picture of him, though there was one of our grandmother, Bobbe, whose real name she had forgotten. I pondered that Zayde was a very strange name, I have never heard before.

But, then I remembered that Hanna and Mama have been talking about him when I was a child, telling funny stories about him, and yet, that they always had been crying. They must have loved him very much! I was so sad that I never got to know neither him nor my grandmother.

Actually, I did not know any other relative but Hanna. When there had been so many children of our grandparents, why did I never get to know any one else?

Hanna, too, had several sisters. I only knew that her mother died at childbirth when Hanna was the only one at home and only fifteen years old. I knew that all but one besides her had married, but I never met them.

They also have had one brother of whom all the sisters were very proud and terribly saddened when he committed suicide as a teen-ager.

I just knew that she had stayed with one sister after she left us right after the war, and that this sister had long since passed away.

Was the only justification for never meeting any of them that I was so much younger than all of them? Or was there something else going on I was not supposed to know about?

Again, so many unanswered questions...

◆   ◆   ◆

Since I had a tubal ligation after Vita's birth, I at least did not have to worry to have more children. It had made me wonder though, why my husband would not rather have gone through having a vasectomy...Why was it that always the women are being punished? That was the feeling I had after letting it happen. But then, I was very tired...

I tried to play with the little ones, but only too soon I noticed that I was not any good at that. I did not know how to play! Was it because I did not have a childhood?

I let the nannies take care of the playing, I tended to sewing and knitting for them, shot home movies and made lots of photographs of my children. And I did drawings of them. Little portraits, nothing special, the kids would not sit still anyway. I only accomplished few pencil sketches which I gave to my husband for his birthday.

And Hans was right in his prediction that I would be working as a pediatrician. I was always reading everything I could get my hands on pertaining pediatrics and I would most of the time know exactly what was wrong when one of the children got sick. Then I could treat them, nourish them back to health, read to them and tuck them in at night…

Otherwise I painted a lot and was happy when little Nele would come every so often into my studio and watch me in action. She started to draw at a very early age and showed genuine talent.

All the kids were very well taken care of, especially by Hanna, who took them out into the garden and watched them play in the sandbox while the other nannies and helpers would keep the older ones occupied.

There was always a lot of laughter and noise in and around the house, many friends visiting with or without their parents and there were a lot of sleep—overs that never caused any trouble, only left fond memories.

◆   ◆   ◆

Hans and I now attended several social activities. He had also started to play Bridge which I learned quite some time ago. Now we would either play together with other couples at their homes or have them over at our house to play.

◆   ◆   ◆

When little Vita was almost two years old I got sick and lost a lot of weight I could not afford to, because I had already no more than a little over a hundred pounds. I could not eat, had biliary colic, was diagnosed to be a *stone-rich* woman, which, in this case, was no fun at all, and I had to have a cholecystectomy, i.e. my gallbladder removed.

After recovery I still did not feel well. Two months later I was diagnosed with cervical cancer and had to have a hysterectomy. I was only thirty-one.

Hans was even more frightened than I when the biopsy had come back positive. This time I had to stay in the hospital four weeks, could not be home when my oldest of the little ones, Mone, as we called Simone, would turn six.

She had already begun school a year before and was looking forward to celebrate her birthday with several classmates.

At that time I had learned to appreciate that one of Hans' half sisters lived close by. She and her two daughters had visited with us at all the preceding birthdays of the children, and her husband who was a handyman of all trades, had done a lot of improvements at our properties.

It just so happened that Elizabeth's younger daughter had her birthday at the same date as Mone. She was three years older, though, and Elizabeth was a natural with children. She always knew how to entertain them and make them feel good. She let Mone invite some of her friends and would have a big party at her place. I was very grateful for that and so was Hans.

But when my husband came the next day to visit me in the hospital, he was the bearer of awful news: early that morning our so beloved Hanna had died.

Again I could not say good-bye, not even attend her funeral.

All the children were totally bewildered, stump in grief.

All but the very little ones understood this time that Hanna was dead, was gone forever.

It was five years after my mother had died and then the three little ones were not even born.

I later learned that one of Hanna's sisters had arrived to take all her possessions, but did not take care of the funeral. So, Hans had put her to rest close to my mother.

Now I really felt to be an orphan.

I had a family of my own, but nobody anymore who knew me as a child. And nobody who could ever shed light on all the mystery regarding all those unanswered questions about my heritage.

◆   ◆   ◆

Before I had fallen ill, Hans had fired our cook, he did not like her way of preparing our meals. No one could measure up with Hanna's cooking anyway. But Hanna had agreed to only take care of it once in a while. She rather would watch the little ones and sing lullabies to them.

After her giving up the cooking responsibility, it was up to me to do the job. I actually liked to cook; I was used to doing it during my childhood, but never for such a big crowd. However, Hans was always appreciative of my meals and I got somehow used to being a housekeeper.

My husband loved to work with me in the kitchen, doing all those little chores before the real cooking process would begin.

Just preceding my second surgery, our kindergarten teacher whom we had hired several years ago, was to get married and left.

While I was still recuperating in the hospital, Hans had asked Elizabeth to fill in and take care of the children after school and oversee the recently hired young nannies.

The cooking was done by an aunt of Hans who would stay with her husband in the guest house.

How different was the welcome back when I finally came home again! Hanna always had made a special dinner, all my favorites when I would come home after having a baby. Even after my first surgery I was allowed to eat whatever I wanted and Hanna had taken care of it.

Oh, how much I missed her! When I got home this time, it felt like I had come to a different place. Everything was incompatible: no welcome cake, not even any preparations for dinner in progress.

Although all of my family was happy to have me back, yet everyone was waiting for me to decide what we should have for dinner! I was still so weak from all the treatments, and that's what they expected me to do?

I was almost about to ask my husband to take me back to the hospital, I remember. I was so disappointed, did not openly show it though. Somehow I managed to get dinner ready with an empathetic Hans by my side.

He tried to explain why he could not get aunt Lina to prepare anything, she was just insecure, did not know if I would take to her way of catering.

She would help me in the following weeks until they had to leave again and be more attentive to our taste.

◆   ◆   ◆

Elizabeth now became my constant ally.

In the mornings she would take the little ones to Playskool, Vita was now almost two and a half. They normally did not take kids under the age of three, but with us one was willing to make an exception.

The children had to be picked up by noon. Elizabeth took care of that, too. Now we employed only one nanny who would live with us. I still had a live-in-maid and some who would come daily.

Elizabeth had to think of her family too, nevertheless, she would be there every morning and stay until after she had picked up the children from school.

◆   ◆   ◆

Hans and I now had to do a lot of traveling with the Lions club, since he had become the governor of his district. We would get to see a lot all over Western Europe, the United States and Mexico.

That was the time when Hans decided that it would be the best solution to ask my first maid and her family to take up residence in our guest house, to have someone at home to watch out when we were gone.

She was the one whose wedding had been held at our residence many years ago, who still had helped with the laundry after she had already her own family with three children, but eventually had to move because her husband had been stationed at an other town.

Now her husband wanted to retire from the military, and they were only too glad to stay at our home until they would find a permanent apartment in Hamburg.

Sandra just had started first grade, and only Tobias and Vita were still in kindergarten which preschool is called in Germany.

Elizabeth was our most reliable associate, though. If it only had been possible for her to be with the children all the time! We would have felt so much more comfortable, leaving our most precious gifts in her care. I always was heartbroken when I had to depart.

But Hans was adamant that I accompany him, especially on overseas trips. Those trips were never long, mostly fourteen days. To me those two weeks seemed always endless…however, I enjoyed to being introduced to the United State of America.

Hans made up for those childless trips by taking us all to the Canary Islands which was evidently a wonderful experience for the children.

◆   ◆   ◆

There was still an other issue we did not agree upon: my husband still did not feel at ease at social events with dancing, but he did not want me to dance with anyone else either.

He did not openly show it though, only wrote me little notes which I would find the next morning on my night stand, telling me about his jalousies, his strange feelings he could not suppress and which took him so far over the edge that he rather would die than see me in an other man's arm.

Even when his intellect told him that it was just innocent dancing, something he was not good at, he could not rid himself of that sentiment which would overwhelm him.

In his very subtle way he was able to put a seed of guilt into my mind, that it was my fault, my wickedness that caused him pain!

From then on I made up excuses to not have to go to those parties and dedicated my time to tend to the kids, to paint and read.

◆　　　◆　　　◆

And I finally had time to go through my late mother's things which had been stored away for almost eight years.

I thought I might find some threat to her and my heritage by looking through pictures and papers, Cousin Hanna had brought with her.

But I definitely was not prepared for what I did discover:

There was a note, several times folded and worn out looking, which stated that Tate had been taken to a concentration camp, probably in *Mauthausen.* It referred to the warning this former maid of ours in Vienna had given Mama, when we had to leave so suddenly. It explained that she had watched those Nazis forcing their way into our house and taking my father, wearing the Star of David on his jacket and then shoving him onto an open truck that was already packed with people, all with the yellow star. The last lines of the note told my mother, that the Doctor looked very pale. She wished my mother all the best and signed it Gisella.

In her own words, Gisella wrote:

Frau Schneider, Sie duerfen nicht heimkommen. Die haben Ihr Gemahl abgehohlt, aufn Wagen geschoben wo schon viele Menschen waren, alle mit dem Stern.

Der Herr Doktor sah ganz weiss auss.

Mutter sagt die bringen alle nach Mauthausen.

Alles Gute
Gisella

That was why she did not want Mama and me to go back to our house. My father was taken away; wasn't that the feeling I had as a little girl when we had to leave our home?

I remember reading that note over and over, realizing that Mama must have done the same all those years since we left Vienna!

So, that was it: my Tate was Jewish and the Nazis had killed him like they had so many millions with him!

But what about my mother? Was she Jewish too? Was that the reason for all those *traditions*?

Oh, how excited I was!

Everything would be totally different. I needed to find out!

I found one of Mama's documents that showed her first name and maiden name, not her married name. And for her parents' names there were question marks, nothing was written; she was presumed to be an orphan. Was she really an orphan? I did not know that. Poor Mama, growing up without parents! No, that could not be true! She and Hanna had talked a lot about my grandparents. What about the question marks? Was that true, did she not know her parents' names, was she too young to remember them? I could not believe it!

How then did she know that cousin Hanna was her sister's daughter? This did not make sense to me!

Again so many new questions…

If I only had thought of Mama's journals at that time! There must have been still some from my childhood. Why did I not think of it?

But would it have made a big difference then?

I don't know the answer to that. I could not even deal with the knowledge I already had.

This made me remember something, cousin Hanna had written in one of her letters to Mama, when I was so desperately looking for clues in my childhood years. There was being mentioned that all of the doctor's family and his mother's relatives, the Rosenzweigs, were gone...

I did not pay much attention at that time. I did not know who the Rosenzweigs were. I do not even recall why this incident crossed my mind at this day. Then it dawned on me: those must have been my father's families, his fraternal, the Schneiders, and maternal, the Rosenzweigs! But what now! What should I do?

How should I explain to my husband that I was definitely of Jewish origin? To him, who had not known anything what had happened during the terrible Nazi era...?

Why had my mother lied to me all those years, even after the war, when the facts of those horrifying crimes had become common knowledge?

Was she ashamed to not have informed me earlier? Was it in her opinion too late to tell, after I was married to a non Jew and had several children? Why didn't she tell me before I got married, then?

But couldn't it also have been that because of her experience with anti-Semitism she was convinced that there would never be an end to it? Did she not say so when I was a child?

Why was everything so complicated, so difficult, such a tangle?

It felt like being part of one of those science fiction movies that just had become trendy, only that this one was not futuristic, but part of my past, and I could not find my way out of this labyrinth.

I looked for more information, facts, papers; I could get any clue out of, but in vain. There was no birth certificate, no proof of marriage of my parents. Only this multi folded note and my mother's identity card with the name Emma Grilat on it. There was nothing else. Nothing that showed her name as Emma Schneider. But was not my father's name Schneider? My maiden name was Schneider, Liva Rena Schneider. That's what it said on my marriage certificate! Where did my mother hide all her other papers? I finally got tired of all this mystery for now. I had a family to take care of and a husband whom I could not tell and ask to solve this puzzle...

◆   ◆   ◆

By now Tobias had already skipped one grade and was in Sandra's class. And our baby would start school!

Our maid's family had found an appropriate apartment and there was no need for a nanny anymore.

We had still our secretary whom Hans took with him to the University for Private Practice also working in her office in a separate small building on our lot.

Elizabeth would still come every day and we only had a few people who did the usual housekeeping jobs. I always did the cooking, it kept my mind off all those unanswered questions and unresolved urgent issues.

Hans was now equally involved in school—parents issues as he was in Lions related matters.

He even had started to set up his practice in our guest house and was seeing patients there only on certain days when his obligation at the university would allow it.

◆   ◆   ◆

Right after our little Vita had started first grade, Hans suffered a heart attack. I found him by chance in the bathroom, after I had looked for him twice before.

He was unconscious and I tried to revive him until the paramedics finally arrived. He was taken to our small suburban hospital; there was no time to get him to the university hospital.

Rafael stayed with the little ones; Tim came with me to the hospital where Elizabeth was already waiting.

We waited for quite some time.

Finally a young assistant physician came and gave us the terrible news that there was nothing they could have done, my husband had died!

Elizabeth took me in her arms and started crying. Tim cried uncontrollably, but I was only stunned, totally numb, in shock, could not shed a tear!

The next days are something I cannot remember much about. I did all my usual work, and then I was sitting, just staring into nowhere...

Elizabeth took care of all the funeral arrangements, let the university know and was trying to comfort the children, who really were too young to lose their father.

Was it my fault? Did I cause him so much heartache, that he could not bear it anymore and rather give up?

Then I would get angry at him for leaving us. Now I had four little ones and three teen-agers to rear by myself.

Why did he do that to me?

I would ask God what the purpose of this was. I did not get, not even expect to receive an immediate answer.

Somewhere deep inside I felt that I might learn some day the explanation to all my WHYs.

◆   ◆   ◆

Until then I would have to do my very best to be father and mother to my children. If I only knew, how!

All of the sudden I had to deal with everything. With issues I was not in the least prepared to deal with, like mortgages, insurances and to break up the practice. With other financial matters I have dealt already for a long time starting soon after we got married.

Now we did not have Hans' income from his private practice, and the pension I would receive was relatively small.

I could not start working as a general physician I did not want to be in the first place. I should have finished my five years of specializing to become a pediatrician…

All those should haves did not console me and did not make it any easier to get on with my life as a mother.

I was grateful for Elizabeth who came to be with us every day. She even started to become a homemaker for us. We tried to teach the children to take care of their own rooms, their pets and do some yard work, because I had to let go most of our employees, including the gardener, in order to keep the house as long as possible.

I tried to get involved in school affairs, but just figured out early enough that I could not fill my husband's shoes.

When I would try to help my kids to better understand subjects, some of them were not that good at I learned that I did not have the patience for longwinded explanations. I would easily get nervous and intolerant when they did not grasp, not comprehend completely right away which, in turn, irritated them and finally lead to tears. Sometimes on both sides of the table.

I was not sensitive enough to my children's emotional needs, just wanted them to get good grades and become responsible adults.

My mind was more or less occupied with the idea of finding my own spiritual identity.

One thing that gave me comfort though, was that I knew I could trust my inner voice that had always known that I was different, and now I had the reassurance that I at least was part Jewish.

I did not know any Jews in our neighborhood, maybe there were none left. Or the ones who had been hiding were still too afraid to openly admit it. None of my children's school mates was admitting to be Jewish. There were even now, so many years after I was in school, only two religious beliefs to choose from, either Catholic or Protestant. Baptists or Methodists were considered sects.

Sure, the Holocaust was a big issue in my children's schools. Reading the 'Diary of Anne Frank' was mandatory in every German school. Yet to many people it was just an other story, a story, not a true life experience.

And then there were those ones who outright denied that the Holocaust ever happened...

A new political party had been around now for a while. They called themselves *the Republikaner*, did not have anything in common with the American Republican party though.

They were a far right, fascist group of people who not so secretly tried to bring Hitler's image back as a positive one! Unbelievable!

Most people had left the churches, because the government was charging taxes, called *Kirchensteuer*, depending on people's income. This tax was supposed to pay for the churches and their clergymen.

I tried to find out as much as possible in literature, but mostly was referred to the *Old Testament*, which was not enough for me. I had studied in philosophy class about the whole variety of religions, with Judaism barely mentioned.

The Nazi definition of a Jew was, that anyone, who had two Jewish grandparents was considered Jewish...

◆   ◆   ◆

I again had to delay my research.

My children had to be my priority for now!

I thanked God that they were all healthy, beautiful and knew how to use their brains.

After Rafael had come back from the US, where he was as an exchange student, he started to study to become a technical engineer. He had an obsession with motor cycles since he was twelve. Now he wanted to design new machines. I got him a used car and sent him to a technical university in southern Germany. All the other kids were still in school.

Tim wanted to study at film school in Munich after his graduation. He was a very good photographer and made the most amazing home movies.

He got an early start on his hobby; he was only eleven when he would shoot the first '*special effect*' movies, using his siblings as actors. He had a vast imagination; his resourcefulness was broad and never-ending. He would entertain at all the birthday parties of the other children and always was a big success.

Nele knew from early childhood on that she wanted to study art. She really had such a lot of talent, that even Hans could be convinced that this was her calling.

Too sad, that he never got to know if she made her dream become a reality!

Mone could not decide what she wanted to be, she had too many different options and talents. She was a very good writer, could act and sing, but finally started journalism, comparable religion and ethnology, was writing and acting on the side, though.

Sandra was the only one interested in studying medicine. She still had a way to go until her graduation. She was in an accident with fifteen, which left her to have several surgeries and miss school a lot.

Tobias had skipped another grade and was now by far the youngest in his class which nobody seemed to notice. He was tall for his age and very mature. His interests were many. He was a very good student; there especially did he enjoy mathematics and all sciences without neglecting the other subjects. But in his free time, and he sure had a lot of it, he ventured with his best friends to watch rare birds and to roam around in the woods. Yet his favorite hobby was to build sound boxes and create computer programs.

He never gave me any trouble, but as a result, he got the least of my attention.

In hindsight I am very sorry about this fact, because we never developed a close relationship. My biggest concern was always given to the ones with problems, how many or for whatever reason, be it health or school related issues.

Mone and he had a very special connection and later he would grow closer to Nele also.

Vita had become a very introverted child in school. At home she was always treated as the baby who was too young, and immature. Although the four youngest were only one year apart. I sometimes even contributed to that which made my little girl very self-conscious.

She loved animals and was very sad, as were the other girls, when I had to sell our three horses, including the trailer in which we used to load them to attend tournaments.

We had purchased them one by one about two years before Hans passed away. I could no longer afford the costs for the stables and care taking at the horse farm.

We still had quite a few dogs and cats, and it was not always the easiest part for me to get the four youngest kids to feed and clean them.

Vita had many hidden talents, she would write lovely poems and stories, but mostly kept them to herself, too shy to show them openly.

It was only when we were on vacations together, that she sometimes let us know what a beautiful voice she had, singing the latest hits and imitating other child singers.

◆   ◆   ◆

Tim was barely twenty when he left for Los Angeles to become a screen writer.

Meanwhile Nele had started to study graphic design and came only home on weekends, until she moved in with a roommate to live closer to her university.

While on a trip to France with her art class, she discovered silk painting, fell in love with this wonderful art form and convinced me to start painting on silk also.

And I loved it!

I had been painting all the years prior to that, but only when time would be available and I was not too occupied with child issues.

But now I had to force myself to perform my duties as a mother in order to not get obsessed with painting on silk.

We had purchased a VW bus after I had to sell Hans' big car, I could not longer stare at and which was only sitting in the garage. I needed a big van in order to get all the children seated.

We called the van *Kermit*, for it was green and Nele had painted all the puppets of Sesame Street on one side of it.

We had taken several trips with all the other children while Rafael was still in the US, and later in southern Germany.

One year during summer break we went to England for a few weeks, another year to Sweden.

Then I wanted the children to see Vienna on our way to Yugoslavia.

I had visited Vienna before, even stayed there for a while, studying with Hundertwasser—by now I had my BFA—and I was looking for any information of my father's family. Again, I found nothing. Later I wrote letters to the officials, also to no avail.

This time in Vienna I tried to find out if I could get intelligence about any surviving family members of my father's, or at least a clue of where and when he was murdered.

Again all my search was in vain. I even experienced animosity, to say the least, at those offices that should have been helpful.

This new wave, or was it still the same old one, of anti—Semitism really shocked me.

I rather would have turned around to Hamburg than spend another day in Vienna. But I could not disappoint the children who wanted to see more of my otherwise beautiful place of birth. Overhearing an expression, while visiting *Schoenbrunn: that Hitler's biggest mistake was to not have killed all Jews!* Made us leave immediately.

◆   ◆   ◆

The day Princess Diana and Charles got married, my four not so little ones and I took a flight to Los Angeles to visit with Tim who had invited us over during the children's summer break.

We would stay in a new hotel right at the ocean in Venice. The kids enjoyed to see their brother in action, introducing them to all his friends and to the world of Hollywood.

Vita, who turned fourteen there, although younger looking, was becoming the center of attention. Everyone wanted to take a picture of her. It was probably the first time that she started to realize that strangers thought her to be beautiful and not a little child anymore. Sandra and Mone were already used to this kind of courtesy.

How disappointed was Vita after this experience when her big brother got her a children's ticket for the movies just to get us in for less!

So, to the family it did not matter, that she was considered an almost adult, here she was still the little kid! She was so embarrassed that she did not want to see the movie at all. The only one totally oblivious to the whole incident was Tobias.

We could finally convince Vita that Tim did not want to hurt her feelings that he only wanted to save some bucks.

He made up for it later when he bought her a very becoming evening gown for our night out to see the performance of Evita.

Mone and I were amazed by the wonderful acoustics at the Hollywood Bowl, where we attended an extraordinary concert, conducted by Zubin Mehta.

Time was too short for all the excitements and we had to leave for Hamburg again.

♦   ♦   ♦

It soon became obvious to me that we had to cut back on expenses in order to keep our home.

This did not sit well with Vita who had become now used to expensive cloths and vanity.

All of the sudden she would turn into a punk making herself ugly looking, coloring her hair purple and skipping school as much as possible, until getting caught.

Even then she would not change, influenced by a new crowd of admirers, she ran away from home, stating later that no one in the family could understand her and her friends.

I could not get through to her, neither could her siblings. I really was afraid to lose her, and did not know what to do.

After she had turned sixteen, Vita one day invited a young man into our house, who was dressed up all in black leather from head to toe, and those parts not covered with that sort of skin were covered with tattoos, his face, his neck and his hands. After telling me his name, without much ado, he told me that he was to marry my baby. He did not ask me. He just told me!

And I told them that there was no way for this to happen! I knew I was playing Russian roulette, when I refused to let them get married. They always could have gone to social services and get their permission, for he was over eighteen. But I had to take the chance that neither of them knew about this opportunity.

And they bought my explanation that they could not marry without my consent.

It definitely did not surprise me the least when a few month later Vita revealed that she now was pregnant and I had to let her marry that rocker.

I still refused, but offered her that if she would choose to have the child; I would be there for her and the baby on condition that she broke up with the guy.

At first she was furious and again ran away. Not even a week later she came back and accepted my condition.

She even promised to finish high school and to start College after the baby was born.

Now I had my little daughter back. And I would have an additional child to care for!

◆   ◆   ◆

The day of teeny Daniel's arrival, Mone, Sandra and I stayed at the hospital with Vita all day long until after midnight when he was finally delivered by Cesarean section.

His little mom was still asleep when the three of us would bath him and put him into his first cradle.

The next day was Tobias' graduation. Nobody was at home that night. We were all celebrating at the graduation party when some one alerted us that our house was on fire!

The firefighters had already taken care of the worst part, but we could not stay in a house that looked as if a bomb had exploded in it. All rooms were blackened by the smoke, several totally burnt out. My beautiful winter garden which ran along the whole side of the house for more than thirty meters looked like a plant and a bird grave yard. All the colorful budgies and so well cared for plants were gone! There was this terrible smell I remembered from my childhood; burned out houses...

Nothing in the nursery could be salvaged. We had to stay in a hotel until I would find a place to live in for the four almost grown kids, the new baby and me.

We did not tell Vita about this terrible situation. She had put so much thought and energy into creating a room for her baby. Fortunately she would have to remain hospitalized for a few more weeks.

We found a house for rent, and Sandra, Tobias and Sandra's boyfriend would paint and furnish a beautiful nursery for our new family member.

Little by little we had to explain everything to Vita, but left the new nursery as a surprise.

When we finally could take our 'two kids' home, it sure was a surprise for the new mom and she was really grateful for all the love and support her family had given her and Danny.

The police never found the cause of the fire! They assumed it to be an electrical malfunction in one of the refrigerators in the basement.

Vita kept her promise and finished high school and started college to become a kindergarten teacher, and I took care of my little grandson when his mom was at school.

◆   ◆   ◆

First we wanted to rebuild our home where all the children had spent their tumultuous, yet wonderful childhood.

However, we came to the conclusion that this might have been a sign to move on.

Mone, Sandra and Tobias had started university and would soon be moving out anyway.

A year later Tim came back from his six year stay in the U.S.A. He went with me house hunting, and we found a very old wonderful townhouse in need to be renovated.

The children all worked together. Rafael, who had changed his future job plans now to become a social worker, would lend a helping hand, as did Nele who already had received her master's degree in graphic design and wanted to open her own studio and start her business.

She had written her dissertation about silk painting. The most amazing thing about that was that she had written and painted it on silk, starting with the silkworm becoming a cocoon, silk threat that was spun to silk, lead us through all stages and was finishing with a beautiful painting.

Nele and I worked together at the beginning, painting onto everything that did not oppose us doing so!

Mostly we painted on silk, but Nele's ideas and talent had no boundaries.

She created the most beautiful silk garments, made applicates to be put onto jackets and sweaters, even painted and therewith totally changed the way denim jackets used to look.

Soon Nele needed more space and rented a big studio and hired several art students as helpers.

◆　　◆　　◆

With Mone being involved in small acting parts and her studies at the university, Sandra moving in with Peter, her boyfriend whom she already knew since high school and with whom she now studied, Tim, Tobias, Vita, Danny and I were the only ones left to live in this new house.

Not for long, however. Tobias had decided to get his masters in economics and to take care of Nele's business, which was expanding pretty rapidly.

He had to move closer to her studio. The three found a nice apartment where they would live together, exchanged their ideas and would not be disturbed by neither big brother Tim, who always wanted them to do some chores they were not interested in, nor by little Danny, who now always wanted to be the center of attention.

They all loved him very much, but had to live their own lives.

Rafael had already settled down with his girlfriend of many years, but had not yet made the step into marriage.

Tim had to travel a lot, meeting with agents and directors, Vita went to college and I was to raise Danny.

◆　　◆　　◆

One day Tim announced that he wanted to go back to the United States, he just could not get to feel at home again in Germany.

Only a few months later Mone decided to visit him, but first had to go to New York to experience the Broadway atmosphere and there she fell in love with the city and one of her inhabitants.

After receiving her master's degree in Germany, she enrolled in one of New York's most prestigious acting schools, H.B. Studios where she would start a new career.

◆　　◆　　◆

By now I had told my children about my Jewish heritage, I was totally unaware that they had this assumption all along. I could not lead them into Judaism, though. There was only one synagogue left standing in Hamburg, an Orthodox very beautiful one.

But now they would become more aware of the new anti-Semitic movement, provoked by the bold, shameless appearance of the skin heads.

Nele and I took a wonderful trip to Italy, just the two of us, and only for two weeks. We traveled in a van, which was also our sleeping quarters, stayed at camp grounds and bathed in the beauty of Tuscany.

Those two weeks are still filled with the most delightful memories of closeness and shared interests with my oldest daughter, I shall always treasure.

Tim would start calling at least once a week to beg me to come over to the United States with Vita and Danny.

We traveled one day in early October to New York City to visit with Mone first.

We noticed right away how different people were reacting to us; everyone was friendly, although nobody seemed to have time to spare.

◆   ◆   ◆

That's when I made the decision to move my two little ones and me to this wonderful country...

I left Vita and Danny in Mone's care and flew back to Hamburg to finalize the arrangements for our big move.

I arrived in Hamburg very early in the morning of November 9, 1989, just when the wall came down!

I did not know what to expect from this unforeseen occasion. It probably would change a lot. At least it was a big win for democracy. Would it be a win for the Jews too? I sure hoped so.

This strange coincidence with the date of the Kristallnacht fifty-one years ago somehow puzzled me.

I did not waste any time pondering, although I stayed glued to the TV for the rest of the day.

◆   ◆   ◆

At a family gathering I told my other four children about my decision, and we discussed the whole situation at length.

I wanted them to take care of the house, my car and to take whatever they might need for themselves.

We were having a party where the feelings were mixed and the emotions not at all controllable.

Then I said good-bye to my children and Elizabeth, instructed a moving company, and within a week I was back in New York.

So many things there reminded me of something I had known once. I could not put my finger on what it was: it merely was some familiarity with smells, objects, kind of deja vu...

This was something I had seen in my dreams: people of all different origins living in one big community; or was it something else I was feeling?

After having walked the streets of New York for several more weeks, having seen all the wonderful museums and getting acquainted with Mone's American love interest, even having tried to teach Danny some phrases in English, the time had come for us at the beginning of 1990 to move to Nashville, Tennessee and begin a new life...

Part II

Panta Rhei
Always in motion
Overall movement
All is flowing
No standing still
Always keep going
No turning back
Never stagnating
Everything is changing
Nothing remains the same
Rolling rivers
Emerging in the oceans
Shooting stars
Glowing in the sky…
And I am still standing on the same spot
With no way to move—but in pain

We moved in with Tim, who had rented a beautiful house in one of the best locations of Nashville.

I right away fell in love with this charming state and this city which later looked to me like a big park.

Everything was different. The people were nice and friendly, they even asked you at the grocery store how you were doing.

That was something totally unimaginable in Hamburg.

In addition to that they would pack your bags and carry them out to your car.

The stores were open twenty-four hours. Not closed at six at night as in Germany and at two in the afternoon on every Saturday. They were kept open on Sundays too. Nobody was doing that back in Germany!

But those were only by-products of our new life.

And one definitely needed a car here. The distances were unbelievable. Everyone had at least as big a lot, as we had had around our old house.

By the end of January the Japanese magnolias had already started to bloom and the most colorful birds could be seen flying around looking for a mate and a nesting place.

It was not yet spring, but it was mild and the air full of sunshine. Soon we could see all those luscious trees and greens everywhere!

Danny was five years old and would be enrolled in kindergarten.

He did not have a good time at the beginning with the kids in the neighborhood. He would be asked by them to come out and play with them only to return a few minutes later in tears telling me that they had spit at him because they could not understand him.

From that time on he did not want to talk German anymore and put all his energy into learning English at kindergarten. Within three months he would speak like a native.

◆   ◆   ◆

Tim had special expectations of us being a family again.

My idea was somewhat contradictory of his.

I had always wished for one time in my life to live alone, independently, not being responsible for anyone else, not even my beloved children. They were all grown up now and I wanted to pursue my own dreams, be my own person, find my own identity and not be attached to anyone.

I got in touch with a realtor and found a nice little house for rent, surrounded by woods and wildflowers.

Tim was not very happy when I told him that I needed to be on my own. He still had Vita and Danny…

Knowing I was acting selfishly leaving Danny and Vita in his care, I felt sorry for them, for he was not the easiest person to live with.

Nevertheless I had to move on. I was so much looking forward to start silk painting again that I could not wait to get all my boxes unpacked.

What a terrible surprise it was when I discovered that all my silks were gone, lost in that huge ware house in New Jersey where everything had been stored after it's been through the customs.

So I had to start from scratch.

◆   ◆   ◆

While waiting for the suppliers to send me their catalogues, I started volunteer work at the Tennessee State Museum as a docent for an art exhibit. Prior to that I had already become a member of several arts organizations in town and made quite a few friends there.

Everyone invited me with open arms. When I had a problem at the beginning to understand the southern accent I gradually got accustomed to it and soon could understand what they were saying however, still far away from speaking this kind of English.

Those three months at my first job as a volunteer brought me a lot more insight into the way of southern living. And I learned that most of the other volunteers were Jewish.

We got along just fine. I became friends with several ladies in spite of my coming from Germany and knowing that many of them must have lost relatives through the hands of Nazi Germans.

I did not yet disclose my own heritage and was still hesitant in doing so. I do not know why…

◆   ◆   ◆

When I finally could start my own business with hand painted silk items, I really became busy.

I loved to work, had the most intriguing ideas at night, and did not have time to wait until morning to put them into action. I just would get up in the middle of the night; climb the stairs to my studio and paint, totally in oblivion of time and space.

Those were the most wonderful hours, listening to music and painting, painting…

Then there were the shows I had to attend, some with my wearable art, the others with framed wall hangings.

Receiving commissions and awards and selling my art at all different locations made me almost become a traveling artisan.

I did not only appreciate the beauty of the state of Tennessee, I also got a feeling for the travel distances and the diversity of the different other cities and states.

It was a wonderful time and experience!

In the year after we came to Nashville, Vita got married to a very handsome and talented young engineer. They purchased their first home and he soon adopted Danny.

Tobias came with his girlfriend from Hamburg to attend the wedding and Simone brought Mike with her from New York, who still was her only love.

It was a very nice church wedding, the first one I was ever a part of. Vita married into a big family. Her husband had two pairs of grandparents still living and Vita had two sets of in-laws.

Now that I was convinced that my two little ones were in good hands I did not feel that guilty anymore to have started to be on my own.

At the beginning Tim was still miffed that his family reunion did not work out the way he had planned. Yet he was pleased with Vita's choice for a husband and a father for Danny. He gave his little sister away and Danny was the ring bearer, a very proud one!

And after all, we lived in the same city not far from each other in different homes though, which made it easier to get along with one another in the long run.

Now I finally could live my own life without guilt.

Besides doing my artwork I still remained a docent for various exhibitions at the State Museum.

◆   ◆   ◆

It was not until the traveling exhibition of Anne Frank's memorabilia was on display in the museum, and several friends had talked about their Holocaust survivals, and lectures had been held by the exhibit accompanying director from Holland, that I could tell my friends about my heritage.

It was then that I really could identify with all the pain and suffering most people had to endure, who somehow made it come alive through that horrific, gruesome time of the genocide, the Shoah.

Although I could not compare my experience with theirs which was beyond comparison, I also have been deprived of having a father, other relatives or a Jewish education.

How could I find out after so many years if there was still some one anywhere in the world who might be a close relative?

Where should I start searching, how could I put all my energy into finding out and still make a living with my artwork?

I received a lot of tips from my friends as to how, but I also knew it would be very time consuming.

First I had to work, save some money and then pursue my urge for doing research.

◆   ◆   ◆

From Nele I received the most stunning news: she, who was always very particular about dating, had found mister right, actually already before we had left, but she did not know it then…and now they had a son, Carl.

She had kept me updated during her pregnancy and now my second grandson was born and I could not be with her! They would come visit as soon as the baby was fit to travel.

It still took almost another year until they came to Nashville and by then Vita and James had a little daughter, Theresa.

Now Tim had another little one whom he could spoil as he had done with Danny before.

When Nele and her family arrived here, they had brought Sandra as special surprise.

When Mone joined us, I at least had my four girls for a little while and Tim would show them around showing off his beautiful sisters.

Even while the children were here, I was working and doing several shows. Nele seemed to be pretty proud of her mom who appeared to be more contented than ever.

But I most certainly knew that she was a much better artist than I have ever been...

We still would find time to be together during their four week stay. And they came to every show I exhibited in.

But four weeks are just like a spring storm, long anticipated and fast over with.

◆　　　◆　　　◆

Life was soon back to normal and my work was getting more exposure all over the country.

There were several invitational shows I had to attend and a very big trade show in Javits Convention Center in New York City which left me very busy.

In the same year Sandra and Peter had their first daughter, Anna, and five months later Rafael and Tridi gave me yet another granddaughter, Marlin.

I was so tied up with my work that I could not find the time to pay a visit there. Or did my subconscious only tell me that? Anyway, I did not go!

◆　　　◆　　　◆

In order to get all my commissions done I was already contemplating to hire a few students whom I could teach some of my techniques to get things finished more sufficiently.

However, I had to at least fulfill all my obligations I had already committed to for this year.

During December we had an artisan exhibit and sale show in downtown Nashville.

Being in charge with staffing, opening and closing the gallery, I also had to take care of the inventory.

There were only four days left until the end of the show, when I was making some copies of our inventory sheets at a local office supply store.

Stepping back from the check out counter, I hit my head and my right shoulder on one of those I-beams, which were placed throughout the store to give stability to the ceiling. Painted white to match the surrounding and the floor, this thing could be easily overlooked.

The truth is I did not see it at all and was knocked unconscious by this collision.

One never should try to overrun a steal beam!

Every one in the store was very helpful, especially after my right forehead started to grow rapidly into a balloon.

Holding on to my icepack I made it to the emergency room of the nearest hospital, where one would diagnose a concussion, but no additional brain damage...?.

When I finally made it back to the show after having taken the following day off, I looked as if somebody had really beaten me up, and then, all of the sudden, I could neither move my right arm anymore nor bend my neck.

My friends all helped to pack and finish up the show and load my car.

My physician referred me to an orthopedist who prescribed physical therapy. I tried to strictly follow the schedule, but my physical therapist soon noticed that my strength was lessening more and more and the pain in my right arm was increasing. At the beginning it was only a stabbing pain as if my funny bone would be constantly hit, no laughing matter, though.

Then my arm started burning really badly as if I would hold it into a fire.

The orthopedist conducted very painful nerve tests that turned out to be normal, prescribed narcotics and other pain killers. Yet nothing helped. The pain would get worse and worse...

I was in agony, did not know what to do, since my primary care physician wanted to make me believe that this terrible pain was only in my head.

Several months later he finally let me see a neurologist, who immediately diagnosed that I had RSD, Reflex Sympathetic Dystrophy.

By now my arm was swollen, had a purplish color and was extremely cold, still burning though, and not to be touched.

He sent me to a pain control center where I was being given different medications and was treated with all kinds of pain blocks, for there is no cure for this condition.

The whole staff at the pain center was highly skilled, compassionate and used to treating people with chronic pain. The doctors, who are anesthesiologists, were very caring, and my psychologist would be the one to help me the most to make it from one day to the next.

I had never heard of RSD before and barely anyone I talked to had either.

Fortunately I had fulfilled all my first orders I had received in New York. But when the follow-up orders would come in I had to let people know that I was unable to carry out their demands.

◆   ◆   ◆

Then the most unexpected happened: my landlord, having heard about my misfortune, wanted me to find a new place to stay or buy his house for an incredible high amount.

Now, in the midst of my pain, pain treatments and accompanying depression I had to find a way and place to move to, but how?

My savings were used up by now for medical bills and I did not know what to do.

Then my artist friends would think up a splendid idea for me to get a down payment for a house of my own, an inexpensive one that I had in mind.

Since I still had a large inventory, they proposed to get a fashion show going with all my wearable art for sale. They sent out invitations for a seated luncheon at a fancy restaurant. Seven models out of the group and friends of them would each wear at least three different out-fits, and at the end of the show handle the sales.

Meanwhile I could not use my right arm anymore at all.

My friends put such a lot of time and effort into this show that it had to be a big success.

And a success it was!

Everything went perfectly, and I was able to make the down pay-ment for my own house, despite my handicap.

My friends helped me pack, got boxes from everywhere, and by the time the movers came everything was already secured.

Due to the fact that I could not occupy my new place right away, one of my friends let me stay in their house for ten days while they were gone.

Other friends would help me get the house a little renovated and painted. When my furniture finally arrived I would let them arrange the rooms as I wanted. But I did not get around to setting up my studio.

The pain was getting worse, spreading over my neck to my left arm, also to my left leg, to the left side of my face, and I was devastated.

Would now my whole body be affected?

I could and would not let that happen!

As I had learnt in the meantime, the pain was caused by an over firing of the sympathetic nervous system, telling the brain that there was still an injury causing this terrible burning, stabbing pain.

Those signs caused me to lose the use of my right hand and arm to begin with. It was just too painful to use it while I was in constant pain. But since I knew now that there was no other reason for the pain, that the pain was, simply speaking, just there, and would not go away any time soon, I had to keep using my left hand and leg as much as possible, even when it was sometimes unbearable!

Now I had a little house of my own, even space for a studio, but no intention, no energy to determine what to do with that special space. I let them put all the *stuff* into that room but I could not establish a relationship with it as I had with my rented studio.

My own person had been an instrument in practicing my art; and it had to be kept fit, according to the functions it had to fulfill. Not to communicate my calling was to surrender my vision to atrophy.

As an artist I had to paint—else the vision would wither away; I was not apt to have it again. Thus my emotions were being held captive inside me, causing my soul to slowly die...

Would I ever be able to paint again?

◆   ◆   ◆

In order to keep my mind halfway sane I started to think up some frustration-poetry.

Those were not positive thoughts that entered my mind at that time, I felt that I had fallen into a black hole and I now would fall deeper and deeper…

I could not even look at my materials, my paints, brushes and silks. The empty frames kept staring at me, my knitting needles were hanging down in a basket, motionless, and together with those balls of yarn I had produced almost a year ago.

I would see those sadly hanging needles as an allegory to my deteriorating physical and mental state.

I was unable to do the simplest household chores, like doing laundry, changing my sheets, cutting vegetables, all those things we take for granted.

Fortunately my new neighbors were all very helpful, assisting me in all outdoor tasks and taking me to the pain center for my nerve blocks.

One of my Jewish friends, who had helped me with my moving business, would come over at least once a week to change my bed sheets and do the laundry. She and her husband always tried to cheer me up. We talked a lot about my heritage and Judaism in general.

But when left alone I was brooding over my situation, agonizing on my future, fret, mope, sulk and worry.

Most of the time the pain was so severe, so excruciating, so hard to bear that I could not even think clearly.

Between my treatments I was only sitting around in self-pity wrestling with my fate and asking God to take this pain away from me.

I never had given up on believing in God, although it sometimes was very hard to just believe and not accuse Him of being unfair.—

I still had the feeling of having some sort of a personal relationship with Him. He was the only one who really knew how I felt, and I could tell Him everything. And I still thought that there was a special reason that this RSD happened to me. I only had to find it!

Sometimes I was in a haze, unaware of my surroundings.

And sometimes I was on a verge of giving up. But there was always a Higher Power that would keep me from taking that last step…

◆   ◆   ◆

I could not tolerate any noise and not be around my grandchildren, for they could not understand what was going on with me.

Just before I had to move, Vita had given birth to a little boy, Henry, and she now had to take care of one more in her family.

Tim was still involved in his writing and traveling and being a good uncle to Vita's kids.

I suspect that my children did not know how to deal with me and my condition. I had much more empathy from my friends than from my own family.

After I was given a medication, actually designed to treat convulsions, I got a little relief from the constantly burning pain.

However, there were very strange side effects connected. Besides being sleepy I would be totally dehydrated, had to drink water constantly. Then my eyes started burning also and were in need of some lubricate.

What mostly disturbed me, though, was my short term memory loss and unsteadiness.

Sometimes I really did not know if I was coming or going.

But several months later, being on a far higher dosage, I got used to this medicine and did not feel like a zombie anymore.

I still remained a hermit, though. I could not concentrate on anything.

That was until Mone arrived here in town to have her baby here and not in the Big City.

Mike had rented a nice apartment for her, but he had to stay in New York City, only visiting about twice a month.

She would help me with little things, and only having her around made me feel less vulnerable.

And when my little granddaughter, Laura, was born she would be taught from the very beginning to not touch my arm, although that was still some time later.

◆   ◆   ◆

I had not heard from Timothy in a while. I knew he was busy as usual, but he had always called me at least once a week.

Time was not an urgent factor in my life anymore. I mostly lost track of it, was happy when I made it through yet an other sleepless night only to count the hours until I could go back to sleep again.

One day, however, I received a phone call from Tim telling me that he had gone back to Hamburg to finish a movie project there. I could not understand why he had done that, he had been happy here, wasn't he?

His siblings enjoyed having him back, he told me and they had made a big fuss about that.

But he did not sound happy, he sounded like he pretended to be happy. Pretending was something he was always good at.

Make believe was his middle name, I pondered. Why had he always been so contradictory, so inconsistent?

Nele had now a second little boy, who was named after his late grandfather, Hans. Big brother Carl was already five, and I had only seen him when he turned one year!

Nele's company had grown a lot. They were selling fashion all over Europe, had expanded their studios over several floors and had built a penthouse on top of the building.

Rafael and his wife had a second little daughter, Jasmine. I had not seen them at all since I came to this remarkable country, and I was yearning to see my firstborn and his family. For now I would have to wait...

◆   ◆   ◆

Several months later I received terrible news: Tim was found dead. He probably had over medicated, taken an overdose of prescription drugs, painkillers he had been on for back pain...

The other children in Germany were totally devastated that they had not seen the signs of drug abuse earlier. Over here the most inconsolable was Vita who had grown very close to her big brother. Danny barely could be comforted at all.

I did not want to believe it, was still awaiting his usual phone call and was about to call him. One time I really did call his number...

I did see his car everywhere on the roads of Nashville, and I do to this day!

A part of me had died with him. Although we used to be fighting a lot, I loved him dearly and I always will...

And I could not go over there to take care of the final arrangements for my son.

What have I done wrong? Why did he do it? We had talked the day before he died, and he sounded like always, upbeat and optimistic that his screenplay 'Project Mankind' would soon become a movie.

Besides sadness I felt guilt, lots of it!

So many new big WHYs…?

◆   ◆   ◆

It was in Timothy's memory that I finally got connected to the Internet. He always wanted me to do it and I was never ready.

Here I learnt that there are so many people affected by this RSD.

There are several websites pertaining to RSD list servers designed only to support people of all ages affected with this condition.

Now I knew that I was not alone with this disease, that there are millions out there, many so much worse off than I, and maybe together we could make others become aware of its existence and finally find a cure to defeat this monster.

Who was I anyway to complain, when there were children out there in agony and wheelchair bound, because their RSD had started in their legs?

One thing we all have in common though, is to share as much information as possible until there will be a light at the end of the tunnel and an end to this suffering!

In the meantime we have to communicate with our friends without faces and try to console each other only by e-mail…

I only could use my left index finger a little for typing, but still enough to get the messages across.

◆   ◆   ◆

Alexandra and Peter, who meanwhile had a second daughter, came for a six weeks stay to Nashville. I was so excited to finally see two more of my grandchildren, Anna and Klara, and to have a little time to spend with Sandra.

Tobias had been visiting already several times, but I had not seen my daughter for six years. She had become a social psychologist, not a physician as she first had planned. She was now leading a home for troubled youth, who had been abused and were very difficult to deal with, always between mental health institution and prison.

Sandra was a natural to encourage those kids to get on the right path again. Peter, although trained as an electrical engineer, worked with her and I was very proud of her and their achievements.

They stayed with Vita's family most of the time, discovered the beauty of Tennessee and took longer trips from here.

They had come in time to be a surprise for Mone's birthday, which made her very happy.

Little Laura got to know her cousins from Germany, and they together with Vita's children, Teresa and Henry, had a lot of fun.

Danny was already a big boy, but very patient with those little ones.

Peter did some badly needed repairs on my house for which I was very grateful.

But when they wanted me to go out for supper with them I had to decline time and time again. Although the medication had taken the edge off of the burning pain, I still was afraid to be touched, which made me very dejected. I felt forlorn to not be able to really hug my little darlings.

Before they left I was in such a gloom that I could not even attend the good-bye supper they all were having, actually not really say good-bye…

◆   ◆   ◆

In order to work through my pain I wanted to read again more seriously. I had loved to read since I could spell the first words and did so all my life.

I would read at night when I could not sleep, but then my concentration was still a big problem.

I was not used to just reading, I was used to read while I was working, either stripping my silk to yarn, or knitting.

Now I was looking through all those hundreds of books I had brought with me.

I could not find Tate's poetry book, yet I knew I had taken it with me. While desperately searching for this valuable memory piece of my father's, I came across one of those journals my mother had let me use when I was a child.

I did not even remember to have packed that when I came over.

I was about to put it away unread again, but on the inside of the cover it said *Sunday school*, which I had not noticed before and I became curious and now I had to look at it more closely.

◆   ◆   ◆

Most of it was written in Suetterlin, this old German handwriting which for me was hard to read.

I had never learned to write in those old German letters.

The more I tried to decipher those letters, to let them become words and sentences, the more amazed I would be.

There first were really some Sunday school themes on those pages. But in-between hidden was life, my mother's life!

Mama had started to wrestle with God in order to find an answer to all those haunting questions she had to carry with her all her life.

◆   ◆   ◆

She was born into a Jewish family in Lithuania before the turn of the century, had several siblings, the oldest sister was eighteen years older than she and got married in that country, as did a second sister. So, she was Jewish! Didn't I know it?!

Her maiden name was *Griliches*, not *Grilat* as stated in the paper I had found so many years ago. Her parents had come from Vilna and those surrounding shtetls, but had moved a lot, had stayed for a while in Memel/Klaipeda, in Tilsit, as well as in some east Prussian cities.

Then something strange happened, as I was reading along, getting more and more intoxicated.

There were other letters, letters I almost could read and understand without knowing the reason for that. As I learned later when I had started to go to the *Yiddish vinkl* at our Jewish Community Center that it was Yiddish what I could read in Hebrew cursive letters.

I do not remember to ever have studied it. It was the language cousin Hanna and Mama were trying to make me believe to be east Prussian.

And soon I would get to know that Tate meant daddy in Yiddish. How spectacular! What else might I find out? I tried to look ahead to find more yiddish words, but there was only one page and a few sentences and phrases in yiddish, and to my dismay I discovered that many pages had been torn out. Torn out probably by me when I was using the journals for my homework!

But I still could put together some facts: My grandfather, whose name I always thought to be Zayde must have had a real name, since Zayde meant grandpa in Yiddish, and Bobbe meant grandma. Didn't I call my grandma in Vienna Bobetchi? Didn't that sound similar?

At first I could not find his name anywhere, neither the one of my grandmother. I could recall that cousin Hannah and my mama had sometimes referred to the name Shlomo.

Maybe that was an uncle or other relative. But then she would call my mama often Yenta as I remember it…

Yet I learned a sad story. A sad story about a very brave woman…

◆   ◆   ◆

Starting on page 14 of my mother's Sunday school journal, it read:

Children, today I want to tell you a story about a very rich and pious man.

The man did have a beautiful house; in the rooms you could see the most precious things. He had enough to eat and to drink. He, too, possessed pretty clothes.

He also had a wife and many children. His name was Peace. He was a Jew.

It just happened to be the day before Passover.

He got closer and closer to the Temple. And many memories of Israel's great history entered his mind. He was the head of a Synagogue in another city.

A Russian captain approached him. He hated the Jews, but at the same time he also feared them.

But this man was a proud Jew, who was not afraid. He knew that God could help in any situation. Neither shyness for people nor fear of an open confrontation should hold him back.

He looked around and saw a lot of people crowding the market place not too far away from him, and there were also many soldiers.

But Peace had not come alone. He was accompanied by his wife and his little daughter, and now he reproached himself for taking them with him for what should have been a happy day.

The captain went to order his soldiers to throw the man into prison because he was a Jew. The children of Israel were at fault for bringing everything bad to all the other peoples on earth. The Jews did not understand it at all.

The captain was a very cruel and merciless individual. He had done a lot of evil to the Jews. He was a murderer.

I do not remember how long it took until the monotone rhythm of the soldiers' boots could be heard. They did not lead him away, but took all his money and whatever else of worth he carried, and beat him to death.

How it happened I do not remember, but somehow the woman died also.

The father and the mother of the child were dead, no!

Fast, as fast as she could, the girl ran away.

The girl was I.

◆   ◆   ◆

On page 16 of my mother's journal I found the following, written in yiddish in Hebrew script:

> I came to the city of Koenigsberg and there into an orphanage. Being there I took an other name. My father had studied at the University of Koenigsberg.
> My family was from Lithuania.

We had lived in Vilna, but also in many other cities and towns.

For quite some time we had lived in Tilsit and Memel/Klaipeda.

Two sisters of mine and their families had been forced out of town, because they were Jewish. *Forced labor camp*?

My sister Hannah was the oldest of all the children and I was the youngest.

Much later I was taught to be a nurse, and was treating many soldiers during the war.

◆   ◆   ◆

Page 20, also Yiddish text:

> In Vienna I became acquainted to a Jewish philosopher.
> He was also a poet and a teacher, a very good man.

We got married in a small Synagogue.

I married my husband with my real maiden name, *GRILICHES*.

My father had told me that this name had a special meaning, *of significant pedigree*.

But now I had become Mrs. Rudolf Schneider.

He had one sister, who was living with her husband in Russia. And an other unmarried sister had gone to Palestine.

My husband had more brothers and sisters, Jakob Ben Isaak, Leah Ruth…

Several years later we wanted to leave Vienna for Haifa, because I wished my child to be born in a safe country.

But we were not permitted to emigrate.

I had the birth of my daughter (*Shira or Sarah*) at home in secret…

When they came to take my husband, we had been visiting with friends.

Gisella did warn me to not go home again.

Instantly, I took my old identity card from Germany…

◆   ◆   ◆

At least now I had the name of my grandfather, *Frieden* in German, means *Peace* in English. So his name was *Shalom.*

Shalom Griliches. But what was my grandmother's given name?

There was no clue as to the town or shtetl they had lived in when Zayde had been killed in one of those pogroms before W.W.I. and Bobbe died also. Mama did not mention if she had been killed or died of some other cause.

My mama was so scared, she was still very young then, she just ran away, made her way somehow to Koenigsberg, where she got into an orphanage, thus the name Grilat. She knew that her father had studied there at the old university.

Here she would become a nurse and was working as such during the war and thereafter. She already knew or learned later several languages and would hide her true identity as long as deemed necessary to her.

She was proud of her heritage, although she could not reveal it. She tried to explain the origin of the name Griliches. She wrote that it was a combination of Yiddish and Hebrew: *graylich yihus* which meant something like being from extraordinary descent. But what descent I could not find out, neither what the occupation of her father was.

I did not find anything about how Mama and Tate met either. Only that they were in Vienna at that time. And when and where they got married is nowhere in those remaining pages. Only some names of my father's family were noted: Milan, Max, Leopold, Ernst, Jakob, Isaak, and female names like Leah, Rifka, Therese and Ruth. One Sister's name seemed to have been Dinah. How they all were related was no where written.

There was only some mentioning about their inability to go to Haifa, where already one of Tate's unmarried sisters lived. The Nazis did not let them out. Maybe at that time my parents did not anticipate that Austria would be taken over one year later...

But something else puzzled me; the name my mother mentioned to have been given to me when she had me at home in secret, Shira—I could not decipher if it was Shira or Sarah written in Hebrew cursive. My mother used to call me always Cherie which I meant to be darling. Couldn't it have also been Shiri for Shira? It war possible, but now I'll never know.

She once told me that she would have named me Wilfried or Winfried if I had been born a boy. Wasn't that a translation for Shalom? Yes, it sure is, as I found out in the library.

Did Mama ever thank Gisella for warning her that those terrible people had taken my father?

How could I find out? Could she still be alive?

Such a righteous young woman she must have been!

◆   ◆   ◆

By now I read a lot about Judaism was invited by a friend to celebrate Rosh Hashanah, the Jewish New Year and went to services with her.

And all the pieces somehow fell together: my mama's strange behavior, like cooking latkes in cod liver oil, the Sabbath ritual, the braided bread and her candle lightening for Chanukah!

Even the eight candles on a Christmas tree made sense now!

Thinking back to an incident in my childhood, I now know why everyone was so astonished at first when I had completed an assignment, which I had received from my needlework teacher. I was to make a dress for a star singer for some school play, and a big star to be carried by this student who was to wear the dress. I must have been about twelve at that time.

For the big star I had bought a sheet of copper, cut it out and, using up a lot of my mother's towels that I put on a wooden board, embossing that copper star. After sewing the dress, I cut out two thousand small stars out of gold colored foil and glued them onto the dress.

It looked very pretty. All those stars, however, were six pointed...those stars must have been the only stars I have ever really seen before, engraved in my memory...

Had I reminded my mama at that time of her heritage?

How much must she have missed her Jewishness and to go to services!

I right away felt at home there!

How must my mother have suffered, being surrounded by non Jews, even lots of anti-Semites, who would have turned us in had they only known!

And never being sure when the right time was to tell me the truth, until it was too late. It was too dangerous. She must have felt this danger still after the war, because she could have applied for compensation from the Germans for the loss of her husband, my father.

This way she saved our lives. I wanted to tell her how grateful I was for that.

On the other hand I was searching for my identity all my life and she must have known that too, remembering all my questions.

Was she so insecure of my discretion if she had told me?

My only guess is that she just missed the right moment.

Could I have received a Jewish education in secrecy?

Could I have raised my children in the Jewish faith? I do not think so! Did my mother keep that in mind when she did not tell me?

I still do not know the answers...

Yet this revelation was very cathartic to me!

I also found the reason for not celebrating even in secret the holiday of Passover as my mother had tried to keep her other traditions somehow alive. It would have been a terrible reminder in a per se terrible time!

I remembered that my mother had talked about having lived in Tilsit for a while. When she told me about it, Tilsit was in East Prussia, but later it became Sovetsk and Russian territory, which it is still today.

Yet I do not recall if she was there with her parents...

There was an east Prussian Landsmannschaft back in Germany and I contacted them, thought they might have some information about my mother's family.

I was totally stunned when I received the answer which stated, that people with *THAT* name never had lived in Tilsit when it still was East Prussia.

They even would send me material about the whole area, everything Germanized in 1938, all the names of those little shtetls with German names.

They would remind me that Tilsit was and would be again a German City, as would East Prussia in its entirety.

Those people belonged to a group that wanted their *Homeland* back, far right winged, pretending to be unaware that the old Memelland and East Prussia belonged to either Lithuania or Russia.

I right away tore the letter apart, but did keep the material.

One could see their anti-Semitism lurking between each and every single line.

How glad I was then that I had made it out of Germany before people like those might have started yet another crusade!

◆　　◆　　◆

Tobias usually came once a year to visit with us. In the meantime he sent me e-mails with pictures of my beautiful grandchildren in Germany.

This year he was already here in February and then he announced in one phone call that he would be back in September.

This time he was to bring his new girlfriend to introduce her to his American family.

We were all looking forward to this joyous occasion. Vita's family picked them up from the air port very late at night.

Tobias and Ines arrived the next morning at my house, and although I had talked with Ines only once on the phone, we both felt as if we knew each other quite well already.

Through my support group on the Internet I had received many new information and treatment suggestions. One new treatment was a cream containing a higher solution of a well known anesthesia. This cream had to be compounded, and I had just found the least expensive compounding drug store in California a few months earlier. My Anesthesiologist is very open—minded, and he prescribed this gel for me.

It made such a big difference! I have to apply it several times a day, but then it really takes most of the burning pain away until I have to apply it again.

I started feeling so much better; that I could go out for dinner with my kids, even have an evening at Vita's with all the children and Vita's in-laws to have a wonderful home cooked meal followed by a slide show of the children when they were really young, including a lot of memories of Tim and their father.

The grown children most certainly enjoyed those colorful reminiscences more than the little ones.

And I enjoyed being able to be around them.

I told Tobias about my incredible findings, gave him copies of my mother's journal to take home for his siblings.

And he promised to look for more of those journals in his attic, where he had stored most papers that had been rescued from the burnt out old house...

◆   ◆   ◆

Even though I am still in pain, still have to take loads of medication, use my cream as often as necessary, and I am still writing with just my left thumb and index finger I have become a different person.

I am attending *yiddish vinkl* on a weekly basis, and enjoy the company of all my friends there. We all try to keep this wonderful old language alive. Isn't this the language all our ancestors could communicate in where ever they lived?

When I told Mone at this year's Rosh Hashanah that this is the Jewish New Year 5759, she responded by saying '*oh, that old are we already?*' which made me really feel good.

I love to be part of my new congregational family at Temple, partake in as many events as possible. And I am not afraid anymore to be touched.

And now I have the possibility to do research on my family history by getting connected to the whole world of my Jewish ancestry through the Internet.

Maybe I'll get as lucky as some others out there, who already found long lost or never known relatives.

◆　　◆　　◆

If it had not been for this condition, called RSD or now CRPS, I probably would still be running through life breathlessly, always in motion there would be no standing still, no time to reflect, no time to search for my identity, no time to look for the truth, no time to really thank God for all I have.

I would have missed out on this opportunity to find my late mother's remaining parts of the journal that has given me so much to live for and finally made me an emotionally restored person, surrounded by family, family in faith and with a genetic interwoven legacy.

I imagine that this was the whole intention of my mother's writing, because the last sentences in her journal are addressing me directly...you will discover in these pages, my child, that my whole life was a search for God.

0-595-25937-5